# Are You a Candidate to Read This Book?

Take this quick quiz to find out. Simply mark Y for Yes or N for No.

___ You can't remember the last time your spouse gave you a real kiss or held your hand.

___ Experimenting in the bedroom means changing the color of the duvet.

___ Your conversations mostly have to do with who needs to pick up groceries and who should take the garbage out.

___ Sex is getting a little ho-hum. You're stuck in a rut.

___ You can predict the exact spot your spouse will touch you.

___ Hopping in the sack with your spouse is just a distant memory BK (before kids).

___ When your spouse gets that Bullwinkle the Moose look, you suddenly have to clean the countertop, the potty, *anything*.

___ Your spouse doesn't want to have sex unless there's no one within a five-mile radius.

___ You undress in the walk-in closet.

___ You're newlyweds, but you're not getting the bang for your buck you thought you'd get.

___ You don't mind crying or getting emotional over a tender moment on TV. But when the tender moment comes between you and your spouse, you're uncomfortable.

_____ Your spouse looks at you blankly when you say, "I was thinking we could try something different."

_____ The get-up-and-go in Mr. Happy has got up and gone.

_____ The last book you read about sex was for your premarital counseling.

_____ You don't talk about what you really desire in sex and intimacy. It's too embarrassing.

_____ You can only make love with the lights off.

_____ The highlight of your day is watching sitcom characters kiss while you sit next to your spouse on the couch eating popcorn.

If any of these topics resonated with you and you marked even one Y, you need to not only read this book but share it with your spouse.

If you want a new sex life by Friday—and not just good sex but wow sex, intimate connection, and exciting communication—this book will help you with just that.

I promise.

Do you want . . .

- To fall into each other's arms and experience sex that's better than any romance movie or novel?
- To know why your spouse does what he or she does, and how to learn to talk so your spouse will listen?
- An intimate connection that extends all day, even when you're apart?
- Straightforward answers to the hottest questions about sex and intimacy you've been dying to know but are too embarrassed to ask?
- To build an exciting love that lasts and grows for a lifetime?

With just a little of your investment and attention to these doable strategies, *Have a New Sex Life by Friday* will reap dividends not only by Friday but throughout your entire marriage. It's the miracle jump start that can turn ho-hum, nonexistent, or even good sex into unimaginably wow sex.

I guarantee it.

Have a New
Sex Life
*by Friday*

# Have a New
# Sex Life
## *by Friday*

**Because Your
Marriage Can't Wait
until Monday**

# Dr. Kevin Leman

## Revell

*a division of Baker Publishing Group*
Grand Rapids, Michigan

Published by Revell
a division of Baker Publishing Group
P.O. Box 6287, Grand Rapids, MI 49516-6287
www.revellbooks.com

Printed in the United States of America

Library of Congress Cataloging-in-Publication Data is on file at the Library of Con-gress, Washington, DC.

ISBN 978-0-8007-2413-9 (cloth)
ISBN 978-0-8007-2852-6 (pbk.)

Scripture quotations are from the Holy Bible, New International Version®. NIV®. Copyright © 1973, 1978, 1984, 2011 by Biblica, Inc.™ Used by permission of Zonder-van. All rights reserved worldwide. www.zondervan.com.

To protect the privacy of those who have shared their stories with the author, some details and names have been changed.

17  18  19  20  21  22  23       7  6  5  4  3  2  1

To my one and only,
Mrs. Uppington.
And to those couples
who long for something more.
May you never settle for "less than"
but pursue the gift of wow sex together.

# Contents

# Acknowledgments

It takes a whole village to raise a child, and the same is true for getting a book into the hands of readers.

Grateful thanks to my editor, Ramona Cramer Tucker; the Revell team, including Lonnie Hull DuPont and Jessica English; and all my Facebook fans, loyal readers and listeners, and seminar participants for their honest, in-the-trenches questions.

# *Introduction*

## *Vive la Différence!*

Why men need women, why women need men, and why a good sex life is worth striving for.

There's a reason you're reading this book. You want more sex, more variety in sex, or, let's be honest . . . any sex at all! Do any of these thoughts sound familiar?

- Somehow I imagined sex would be more satisfying. That we'd be closer as a couple.
- What happened to the tingles I used to feel?
- I always dreamed of a spouse who would pursue me sexually instead of simply waiting until I initiate it.
- I thought romance would be a lot more . . . well, romantic.
- Sex doesn't have any of that va-va-voom I expected. I get more of a thrill taking the dog out for a walk.
- I can't help but wonder, *Is this all there is? Is this as good as it gets?*

- I'm convinced the only time my husband thinks of me is when he wants a little (you know what I mean).
- Whatever happened to all those nice things he did for me when we dated?
- It's hard to be in the mood with two kids running you ragged.
- Sex life? What sex life? I think the last time we had sex was . . . I'm not sure my memory goes back that far.
- I have this unsettled feeling that there's more we could have together—more intimacy. That we're missing out.

If you've thought any of the above, you're not alone. Thousands of men and women feel the same way. And you're right—you are missing out. Marital intimacy, including sexual intimacy, is designed as an incredible, personal act between two committed people that cements a relationship so tightly that no one can get in between you.

Right now what you're doing in your marriage either isn't working enough to satisfy you or isn't working at all. It's time for a change. You two deserve more, and you can have so much more—in just five days. Whether you have a sex life, somewhat of one, or none right now, *Have a New Sex Life by Friday* will reveal how to get the warmth, intimacy, and wow sex you desire.

Some of you are saying, "My spouse? Are you kidding me? To have a great sex life, or any sex life at all, I'd have to find a different partner."

Getting a new sex life by Friday doesn't mean you ditch your spouse. Far from it. In this book, I'll reveal the secrets to how you can have a warm and intimate connection, fabulous communication, and yes, even sizzling sex with the one you love.

That spouse you think is reticent about sex could become a tiger in your bedroom with even a little work on your part. It's amazing what can happen when you begin to see the world through your spouse's eyes, and when you use the principles in this book to get to know that person more deeply than you ever have. As I've counseled couples over the years, using these same techniques, hundreds of thousands of marriages have been turned around. Previously reticent partners of all ages are now enjoying the exciting bonds of marital intimacy, including engaging in passionate sex. You younger readers can be like bunnies in a field in springtime. For those who are middle-aged, don't let anyone tell you that you have to slow down when you hit your forties. For those of you older readers, yes, sex is still possible and wonderful.

By the end of *Have a New Sex Life by Friday*, you'll understand why your spouse is responding the way he or she is and how you can talk so your spouse will listen. You'll have answers to the questions you've wanted to ask about sex but weren't sure who to ask. Five days from now you'll be well on your way to building the kind of love that is warm and satisfying and will last until you're both as wrinkled as raisins. When you're away from each other, you'll still have an intimate connection that drives you to text or call each other because you can't stand not to. And when you're together, you might not even need Netflix anymore for entertainment.

Isn't that a dividend worth investing five days in? And all the gusto you can give it?

Every person's views on sex and his or her background differs. No matter what yours are, this book will expand and challenge your thinking about sex and marital intimacy. Decide right now that you will set aside any preconceived notions you have about what sex is and what it's not. Give these principles and ideas your full attention. Forge ahead for your own sake, your spouse's sake, and your children's sake (if you have them), because this relationship deserves your best.

Not only that, but fine-tuning your connection is a great way to affair-proof your marriage.

Ready to plunge in?

## Men and Women—So Tantalizingly Different

What makes men so different from women—other than the obvious male and female body parts? Here are some differences that have everything to do with how men's and women's brains naturally work. They can both tantalize and frustrate, unless you understand how they work and use them to your benefit to deepen your marital intimacy.

### The way we process language and emotions

Psychology professor Richard Haier of the University of California, Irvine, and his colleagues from the University of New Mexico, who studied brain imaging technology, say there is a big difference between how men and women process language and emotions. When males listen to someone talking, only their left hemisphere is activated. With females, both left and right hemispheres are activated. Such activity, they believe, results in females having stronger language skills.

> *When males listen to someone talking, only their left hemisphere is activated. With females, both left and right hemispheres are activated.*

Male brains are about 10 percent larger than female brains (then again, many men are bigger physically than women) and contain about 6.5 times more gray matter (sometimes called "thinking matter") than female brains. But does that make them smarter? Not necessarily. Female brains have more than 9.5 times as much white matter, which connects the various parts of the brain.[1]

It makes sense, then, that females use language to build relationships and are usually better at multitasking than men since both left and right hemispheres can be simultaneously actively engaged. Men in general find it easier to focus on a single task since mainly their left brain is activated.

When navigating, women are more likely to say, "Turn right at McDonald's and then left at the corner market." Men are more likely to say, "Go east one block, then north three blocks."

Those brain differences apply not only to thinking but also to the way men and women process emotions. "Women are faster and more accurate at identifying emotions," says Ruben Gur, a neurologist at the University of Pennsylvania. Women can also change their expressions and tone more easily.[2]

Is it any wonder that sometimes you and your spouse can feel like you are complete opposites? You truly are. If you're a woman, you can bounce from one hemisphere to another or engage both without batting an eye. If you're a man, you're entrenched mainly in one hemisphere and can only see from that side of the brain . . . until your lovely bride helps you engage that other hemisphere she's so good at navigating.

God Almighty certainly had a sense of humor when he created men and women as polar opposites, didn't he? Yet we're drawn to each other because we need each other in so many ways.

I want to be clear here. I believe with all my heart that men and women are of equal social value and are equally loved by God. However, some people transform that statement into, *Men and women are the same.* If we were the same, there would be no need for one of us. Men need women's multitasking natures in order to make their world go around and to remember key events even in the midst of all-consuming work. Women need men's ability to zero in on a single problem or issue and tenaciously pursue it until it's resolved.

### What we focus on and the risks we're willing to take

Men are possibility thinkers and problem solvers. They tend to focus on the present (*What's the issue that needs to be fixed?*)

and the future (*What if I . . . ?*). Because they focus mainly in one hemisphere, they tend to evaluate what needs to be done and take swift action. They take risks more easily because they are targeted on getting the job done and don't allow relationships to stop them from their trajectory. What family members or co-workers think of their decision doesn't tend to enter the picture as a top priority. Getting the job done is their top priority.

Over lunch, men either think about what they're eating or, if they eat on the job, may continue to focus on the project they're in the middle of. Think of it this way: A man juggles events in life by tossing one apple up in the air and catching it as it comes down. Then, when he has finished with that one apple, he selects another apple, tosses it up in the air, and catches it. With that method he makes his way through all the apples in the bushel basket.

> *Men tend to focus on the present and the future. Women tend to focus on the past and the present.*

We men are simple, streamlined. Much easier to understand and navigate than the more complex, multifaceted female.

Women tend to focus on the past and the present. What happened in the past affects their emotions in the present because they have amazing recall, especially when it comes to details that happened in relationships. That's why, gentlemen, women will remember the one time you forgot their birthday, so you better make it your priority not to do so again this year.

Since women use both left and right hemispheres of the brain simultaneously, they tend to think in realistic detail about multiple tasks that need to be done. A woman lives with a continual checklist in her head.

If she's a stay-at-home mom and wife, over lunch she tends to think, *What should I feed my kids for dinner?* What she eats is often little bites of what the kids eat, in between meeting their multiple needs. Most of the time she's used to eating cold leftovers later, in between the kids' next demands and the calls from her husband, who needs her to pick up something for him when she picks up the kids from school. As she's driving, she's ruminating on what's next on her to-do list: *Do the laundry, go jeans shopping with the kid who grew overnight, put gas in the car, buy a brownie mix and ice cream for the neighbors' get-together* . . .

If she's a wife and mom who works outside the home, she's considering all of those same to-dos, plus she adds her professional workload to that list of concerns: *I have to get that big project done. Maybe if I work a couple of hours every night this week after the kids are in bed* . . . *No, I'll see if he could take the kids to the park Saturday afternoon. If so, I could finish right on schedule.*

Because women have many plates spinning at once, they are usually more cautious in what they do and take fewer risks. They are all too aware of the toll it will take on their family if they aren't as available. Yet, since many women are pleasers, they'll still tend to take on too many projects, because they don't want to disappoint others by saying no. As a result, many women live with guilt for not being able to "do it all."

A woman juggles multiple apples, oranges, and bananas—projects of all shapes, sizes, and flavors—simultaneously and manages to catch them before they hit the pavement and splatter. Truly, women are amazing creatures. I admire them and marvel at all they accomplish every day. But that ability doesn't come without some heavy costs to women personally, especially if the men in their lives are unaware of what they truly do, don't support them, and don't show their appreciation.

### Use of "I" versus "we" language

From the minute boy babies emerge from the womb, they are primed to be independent. That independent edge only becomes sharper as they grow older.

Stop by a park sometime and listen to little boys and little girls interact on the playground. The boys are flexing their muscles, pushing each other around, wrestling to see who's stronger, and saying things like, "I'm bigger than you are" and "My daddy will whup your daddy. And I'm gonna whup you." Girls are playing house, holding hands, giggling, and saying, "What should we do today?" or "We could pretend we're . . ."

Notice the difference between the language? Males use "I." Females use "we." Males are all about getting to the top of the food chain, no matter what it takes. They're not concerned about feelings or emotions; they're focused on getting the job done. Females want to relate to others along the way in life; they're concerned about what others might think of their actions and how they might feel.

> *Males use "I."*
> *Females use "we."*

It's not hard to see where clashes might come as the two genders relate to each other, is it?

### How much we're cued in to multisensory information

Because males are more intensely focused and tightly wired, they become bored more quickly. Their left hemisphere moves faster from object to object (they're not distracted by having both hemispheres moving at the same time, as women are), so they can grasp the full scope of any single project—as well as click the remote control on the television—more rapidly than females. However, it also means they can miss cues or pieces of data along the way, since they take in and sift through far less sensory information than females.

Is it any wonder, then, that males sometimes misinterpret what females say? They haven't taken the time, as females have, to process both the verbal and physical cues to see if that person really means what she's saying. Males take words at face value; women look for meaning and cues behind the words.

*Our preferred time for sex—morning, night, or . . .*

While giving a couples seminar once, I asked, "When do you think men prefer to be intimate with their wives? In the morning? Or in the evening?"

I asked for a show of hands first for morning and then for evening. Interestingly, many of the women raised their hands for evening. The men? They raised their hands for both! When I insisted they pick one, the majority chose morning.

The ladies' jaws dropped, and they stared at their husbands.

One woman raised her hand again. "Seriously, morning? But that's the time when I have morning breath, I'm thinking about the million things I have to do to get out the door, and all I want is a shower. And he wants it then?"

"Exactly," I said. "One flash of your feminine curves as you get out of bed, and he doesn't want to let you go. Think about it. That's a pretty big compliment."

Another woman raised her hand. "We've been married for 17 years. You mean he still thinks that every morning?" She lifted one eyebrow and nudged her husband beside her.

I nodded. "Yup. Every morning."

"Wow," she said with loud enthusiasm, and the other women laughed. The men in the audience gave me a thumbs-up.

When I asked the women when they preferred to be intimate, the men leaned forward, eager for their answer. All the women's hands raised for evening. Not a single one said morning.

Now it was the men's turn to gaze at their wives in shock.

One man, egged on by a couple of men behind him, asked, "So, are you saying that we have to compromise somewhere in the middle, like 3:00 in the afternoon?" He shrugged. "I'd have to take time off work."

"Well," I said, "that would be a fun reason for a vacation day, wouldn't it?"

He grinned. "Yeah, but it would be hard to explain to my boss."

I continued, "All I'm saying is, change it up. Be intimate some-times in the morning to please you, and sometimes in the evening to please your wife. But really, any time at all works, including 3:00 in the afternoon. If you decide to go for the morning, why not brush your teeth and take a quick shower so you're both comfortable and pleasing to each other? Women have sensitive noses and also want to look their best. A few minutes of prepara-tion are good for both of you. Better yet, shower together in your own intimate water park. Mornings are perfect for quickies to draw your hearts together during the day. They don't have to take long, but you'll both head out the door smiling.

"If in the evening, the same rules apply, but you might be able to take things more slowly, especially if you don't have kids, if Grandma has them, or if they're safely tucked in bed and asleep. Dim the lights and add some candles. Remember, the evening is the woman's pre-ferred choice, so, men, think *romance*. I know it doesn't come naturally, but do it for the sake of your wife. I promise you don't have to admit you even thought the word *romance* to your buddies, but your wife will sure appreciate it . . . won't you, ladies?"

Resounding applause broke out.

Later that night and the next morning, a lot of happy couples discovered a whole new perspective on lovemaking. I knew the principles had worked, because many of the couples showed up late for my first session the next morning, and their clothing was wrinkled and slightly askew. They wore ear-to-ear smiles, many were holding hands, and nearly all were sitting a lot closer to each other than they'd been the previous day.

That made me smile all over.

---

**Men and Women, Simplified**

See Dick. See Jane. See Dick and Jane together.

One is nothing like the other.

But each needs the other.

And that's what makes life's merry-go-round so fun.

---

## Two Can Indeed Become One

It would be much easier for both genders to be on the same page if the top three needs of men and women were the same, but they're not. As you learn about the top needs of each gender in the chapters to come and how those can be met on a daily basis, you two can develop a deep intimacy as both friends and lovers—the kind of sizzling relationship that lasts for a lifetime. Two people can indeed become one—the goal you were shooting for when you said your marriage vows.

Is it easy? No, it's not. Then again, does anything truly wonderful in any relationship come with a snap of your fingers? However, the journey can certainly be a lot of fun.

There isn't a day that Sande, my beloved bride of over four decades, and I don't laugh hilariously over our differences. Not only are we different genders, but she's a detailed, perfectionistic firstborn, and I'm a happy-go-lucky baby of the family. She likes things lined up in a row and doesn't like surprises. I enjoy going with the flow and love surprises. The more, the merrier! She's a play-by-the-rules sort of woman. Me? I like to break the rules . . . or at least invent some new ones.

> *You two can develop a deep intimacy as both friends and lovers.*

Sande can also find anything in the refrigerator in two seconds. I'm the one with my head stuck in the fridge door for five minutes, yelling, "Honey, where's the mustard?" for the umpteenth time this week.

Enter *Sandra*, alias "Mrs. Uppington" for her classy ways, who sashays in like a queen and announces, "It's right there. On the second shelf, to the right." The mustard has never moved from its usual spot, she claims.

"But honey, I still can't find it," I spout.

There's an exaggerated *hmmmfft* from behind me. *Sandra* reaches a long, slender, elegant arm around me, moves one item an inch, and voilà! She reveals the once-hidden mustard.

Men, just accept the fact that women will always win at the game of hide-and-seek because of their multitasking nature. We men will continually fail to find objects if they have been moved a quarter centimeter from their original spot. Go ahead and blame that fixation on the fact that you're only thinking with your left hemisphere at that moment.

But you can certainly enjoy the game of hide-and-seek when you chase your bride into the bedroom. You might even want to give a little Tarzan jungle roar to add to the ambiance of the evening.

Bet you anything your Jane will love it.


## Don't Settle for "Good"—Go "Designer"

In your search for that intimate connection, don't just go for good. Go for fabulous, sizzling sex with the one you love.

But there's a catch to getting that kind of sex, and I have to say it up front. The only safe, mutually satisfying sex is between two people committed for a lifetime and within the bounds of marriage. It's what I call "designer sex."

Yes, I know some of you could hardly keep your hands off each other before you married. The intensity and thrill of what was to come probably had a lot to do with the fact that it was "forbidden fruit" in your mind at the time, especially if you came from a background where your parents believed sex was for marriage only. However, when you got married, you experienced a big letdown. Your spouse was not the romantic partner you'd experienced earlier, and that has caused dissonance in your relationship. Even more proof, to my thinking, that there's a reason we're better off being monogamous.

Sex was created by God Almighty to be something wonderful between a husband and a wife—as a way of becoming one in every possible way and solidifying a lifetime commitment. If you don't believe me, check out the Song of Solomon in the Bible—the story of two lovers that details intimately what they think of each other. Read it sometime together with your spouse, follow the road map, and I guarantee it'll heat things up in your bedroom. The fact that God himself is the inventor of passion blows the myth right out the window that sex is dirty or something you don't talk about. God planned sex not to be merely a little bump in the road but a body, mind, and heart-melding experience of "hang on to the sheets!"

So why would you choose to have only good sex when you could have wow, designer sex?

I know it's fashionable these days to live together before you get married. In fact, couples tell me all the time, "We've been married for five years but have been together for eight." And

> *God planned sex not to be merely a little bump in the road but a body, mind, and heart-melding experience of "hang on to the sheets!"*

teenagers and twentysomethings have told me, "Why would I want a dating partner or sexual partner who is a virgin? I want someone who is experienced, who knows what to do and how to make it feel really good."

But let me be clear. I believe that God intended sex—the most powerful glue a couple can have—to take place within the safe boundary of marriage. Stepping outside of that safety zone comes with a price tag that you often don't see until much later in your relationship.

In today's society of live-in relationships and "easy divorces" (now there's a misnomer, because no divorce is easy—someone, most often the woman and children, pays the price), that original and pure purpose is often thwarted. The sad and traumatic results are all around us—STDs, children without fathers in the home, teenage girls with a father hunger who fall into sexual relationships, and lonely spouses with workaholic or emotionally absent mates who find themselves in the middle of affairs. And there is little mention of the emotional and psychological effects of that betrayal of trust, and what that does to a person's relationships both now and in the future. Once you've been burned, it's hard to trust again, isn't it?

You may be married for the first time. Or this may be your second time up the aisle, or even your third or more. You can't change the past. There is no do-over in life. But there is a do-it-smarter-this-time. You can choose right now to change your actions in this marriage. By identifying the minefields of the past and evaluating how you stepped into them, you can map the road ahead with positive strategies for growing your marital intimacy.

This relationship deserves your best; your spouse deserves your best. And an important part of that best is developing your sexual relationship until it sings like a finely tuned choir.

In more than four decades of counseling thousands of couples, I can't think of a single couple who said, "We have a great marriage, but our sex life stinks." Or, "We have a sizzling sex life, but our marital relationship stinks." You can't have one without the other . . . for long, that is. Without sex, your marriage is headed for disaster and affairs. So if you're the spouse who is reticent about having sex because of trauma you've suffered in the past or because you simply prefer couch potato evenings, you should care. Your marriage is on the line. If you don't provide the warmth, intimacy, and sex your spouse desires, he or she will be tempted to find it elsewhere. But you can affair-proof your marriage.

Designer sex that's reserved for the safe boundaries of marriage, based on understanding the needs of both husband and wife, and charged with respect for each other is well worth striving for. Great sex isn't easy; it takes a lifetime to get to know each other's hearts and to view events through each other's eyes. I still learn new things from my wife all the time. Those little surprises and our joyful anticipation of walking through them together is what keeps our marriage new and fresh even after four decades.

*Have a New Sex Life by Friday* is full of surprises—including some basics you should know about sex and your spouse, as well as questions you've always wanted to ask but maybe haven't dared.

In just five days, you'll have the keys to your spouse's heart in hand and be able to develop smart strategies about how and when to open that door.

> *There is no do-over in life. But there is a do-it-smarter-this-time.*

On Monday, we'll focus on women—why women need sex. Why is sex so integral to a woman's life? What stops her from desiring sex? And what does she want most of all?

On Tuesday, we'll focus on men—why men want sex. What do they need the most and want the most in a relationship? And why is foreplay just as important to men as it is to women?

On Wednesday, we'll talk about who is really in bed with the two of you when you have sex . . . and how to kick those intruders not only out of your bedroom but out of your house for good.

On Thursday, I'll reveal how you can make love with words, why that is so critical to the health of your marriage, and why words can be the best sexual tool in your marital tool belt.

Friday is "spice things up" day, where you get to plan some fun experiences to bring new zest to your sexual relationship.

The "Ask Dr. Leman" section contains straightforward answers to the hottest questions couples ask about sex and intimacy. You can use them any way you want:

- Look up the topics you're currently wondering about for some real-life questions and time-tested advice. Then ask yourself, *How can I adapt the advice to my own situation?*

- Read a chapter and then flip to the Q & As for that chapter.
- Skim the Q & As for a marital intimacy crash course.
- Use one Q & A per day to jump-start discussion between you and your spouse.
- Use this book for a weeklong seminar for couples' groups or for an eight-week study group.

I'm sure you'll come up with your own ways to use *Have a New Sex Life by Friday*, so have at it. It's the kind of book you can read by yourself, but wouldn't it be more fun to snuggle in bed with your spouse? Reading together will kick off wonderful dialogue and, I hope, a lot of exploration. So read a bit, and then let your fingers do the walking over that wonderful map of your spouse's body.

In the epilogue, the best night of your life awaits. This is when you jump-start the dead battery, revive the ailing engine, and rev up your sex life to full throttle.

I promise it'll be fun.

You'll go to sleep with a smile.

You'll wake up with a goofy grin.

And you'll want to do it all over again.

# Monday

## Why Women Need Sex

Why sex is integral to a woman's life, what she wants most of all, and what stops her from wanting sex.

"I have a question for you men. I want you to visualize the answer in your mind," I told an audience of over 3,000 couples in the Midwest. "How long is your wife's clitoris?"

There was deathly silence in the place. Now, if I would have asked about the penis, there would have been a lot of joking, nudging, and whispered exchanges about the length of that appendage from the male specimens in the room. But talk about female genitalia, and suddenly people get uncomfortable.

"I love silence," I said, and everyone laughed. I held my fingers up half an inch apart. "Are you thinking of this number?"

There was a wave of nods across the auditorium.

"Actually, the answer is . . . nine inches."

Disbelief scattered across the faces in the audience.

"Yup, the clitoris wraps right through a woman's body. It's why, when the clitoris is stroked, her response can be so great. Lots of body parts are involved."

So, gentlemen, when you touch her clitoris and bring her to orgasm, the clitoris isn't the only part of her body that's happy. That warm flush she feels spreads all throughout her body and makes her more eager in her lovemaking. And that pays extra benefits for both of you.

The saying "Happy wife, happy life" is completely true. If you want a happy life, including a wow sex life, you'll take lots of time for foreplay. But foreplay to men and foreplay to women often have very different meanings.

For example, in my home I've learned that foreplay means cleaning the kitchen. Not only do you clean the kitchen, but you also wipe off the countertops. That's part of the deal. And check this out. You also have to put the toaster away. As a man, I have to ask the question, why put the toaster away when you're going to use it in less than 23 hours? But as one smart person said, "If Mama's happy, the whole family's happy." That's the truth.

Over the years, I've learned that part of being a good mate is knowing the quirks of your spouse and flowing right along with them. My role isn't to argue the thesis of putting the toaster away; it's simply to put the toaster away, because it's important to my wife. Sande is a firstborn, and order and neatness are very important to her. If they're important to my wife, they need to be important to me.

So I dutifully put the toaster away.

## Why Sex Is Integral to a Woman's Life

A lot of couples who come to me for counseling are stuck in a rut.

"He's not romantic enough," the wife says, "so I don't initiate sex."

"I can't think romantically if I don't get enough sex," he says.

The only antidote to that dilemma is putting each other first. Then even a dull or nearly dead marriage can be revitalized and more passionate and exciting than you can ever imagine.

Sex is integral to a woman's life. She just may not realize it yet. A lot of women have shared with me the very bad advice their moms gave them on their wedding day: "Just lie back and let him enjoy himself. Sex is something guys need, so you have to learn to put up with it." What a terrible view of the most intimate experience that God created between a man and woman committed to each other for a lifetime! If you grew up with that view of sex, no wonder you'd rather do the dishes than enjoy your husband's attentions when he's in the mood.

Fulfilling sex isn't about going through the motions only because it's something guys need. Sex for a man who doesn't see his wife sexually fulfilled is like a woman trying to talk to her husband when he's reading the newspaper. She craves conversation and tries to engage him, but his non-response or grunts, at best, don't satisfy her need for interaction.

> *Sex for a man who doesn't see his wife sexually fulfilled is like a woman trying to talk to her husband when he's reading the newspaper.*

Choosing to marry means you also choose to put your partner first, before your own needs. Sex is as important to a man as affection and emotional closeness are to a woman.

Most women say, "Yeah, I get that. Sex will never be that important to me. I really would rather cuddle." But that's exactly why it's important to put your partner first. Do you want a man who will stay with you for a lifetime? Who will actively engage with you and your family? Who will listen to you as you talk about things that are important to you? Who will care about what you care about? Do you want him to go to work smiling and thinking, *I'm the luckiest guy on earth to have a woman like her?* Do you want the kind of guy who would take a bullet for you? Who will even do the dishes and the laundry too?

---

**Real Women Talk**
*What I Love about My Husband*

- He's happy for me when I do things with friends and pursue activities I like.
- He found my secret stash of Oreos. Instead of giving me grief for breaking my diet, he drew a smiley face on it and wrote, "Enjoy yourself."
- He takes care of things like the spider under our fridge and the garbage every week.
- After he works out in the garage, he comes into the house to flex his muscles . . . *for me.*
- He supports my desire to use my skills in the workplace and helps out with the kids.
- He brings me a single flower just because.
- Every night he tells me one thing he considers special about me.
- He takes his time making love to me, and we don't always have to go all the way.
- He texts me from work so I can enjoy the highlights of his day with him.
- He does little things during the day to show he's thinking of our family and wants to help out—like getting the oil changed in the car over his lunch hour or picking up milk after work. He doesn't expect me to do everything just because I'm at home with the kids.

---

But it isn't only women who should be putting their spouse first. Husbands also need to put their wives first. Here's what I mean. When a man arrives home from work, what's the first thing he naturally thinks about? I'd bet you a million bucks it isn't, *I can't wait to talk with my wife for an hour about all the blow-by-blow details of her day and mine.* No, all he wants is to change into those comfy sweats, scarf down some dinner, and start channel surfing . . . with maybe a shower mixed in there somewhere. But if he loves his wife, he must choose to put her needs first, before his desires.

34

## What a Woman Wants Most of All

I think God Almighty had a great sense of humor when he created woman as woman and man as man, then commanded them to come together and become one. The top three needs of a woman are affection, communication, and commitment. Ironically, those are the things that most men are very bad at. But when a man understands and meets a woman's needs, and a woman understands and meets a man's needs, oh, the beautiful music they can make together!

### Affection

Every woman longs for her man to reach into her heart and fill it with affection and romance. As soon as any man sees, hears, or thinks the word *romance*, he automatically thinks *sex*. But that isn't the primary thing a woman is looking for. She wants to know that her man chose her as his bride not just once but continues to choose her every day above anything or anyone else. She longs for her husband to think of her not only when he wants to be intimate in the bedroom but throughout the day, even when he's at work or at a football game with his friends.

The man who walks in the door, sees how exhausted his wife is, and helps out with dinner and the dishes deposits affection in her love bank. If he puts the kids to bed so she can take a long, relaxing bath, he deposits more affection. And if he sneaks in and gives her a foot rub in that tub, washes her hair, and combs it for her, he'll fill her love bank to the brim.

When a man does things like that, he's saying to that woman, "I value you. I love you. Bringing you pleasure gives me pleasure. I care about what you care about." When a man asks a woman's opinion, he's saying, "I value your thoughts. Your opinion is everything to me. I want to tap into your multifaceted brain." Now that's the kind of affection that makes a woman purr like a kitten. It's female Viagra. Even better, that dose of affection won't wear off. Women have long memories for details. A week from now, that woman will be happily telling her girlfriends about how wonderful her husband is for doing those things for her.

Every day, wives spend a lot of time doing tasks that are seemingly endless. Not many people praise her for doing the laundry, cooking, doing the dishes, or finishing a project at work. That's why her husband's affection is critical not only to the health of their marriage but to her emotional well-being overall. She needs to hear what she means to her husband—that she's attractive and desirable, that he noticed her new hairstyle and complimented her clothing.

Little things bring women pleasure. My wife loves to get a pedicure. "It's pure pleasure," she says, "because they massage your legs and feet." So, gentlemen, if you've got the bucks to do so, treat your wife to a pedicure every once in a while. Or provide the service yourself with some warm, soapy water, a scrub brush, and a bottle of lotion. That lotion will do double duty on your hands too, so they're softer later when you touch her delicate parts.

The point is, treat your wife as the special princess she is. Do things to please and pleasure her. If those things move you toward the bedroom, wonderful. But don't show affection to her only to get her into bed. For her to enjoy sex, there has to be an atmosphere in your home conducive to lovemaking.

Women aren't like men. Men get excited at the drop of a pin. A little jiggle to your wiggle, and all of a sudden your husband, who had no thought of sex a second ago, is more than ready to go.

You spot that Bullwinkle the Moose look and are frustrated. "How could you possibly want sex? We just had it last night. You remember that?"

"But honey," he says, "that was hours ago."

Sex is not centered on a woman's vagina. It begins in her heart, through her husband's care for her and his understanding of what she thinks and how she feels. You can pursue the physical act of sex with great gusto, but it won't be ultimately satisfying to either of you until her affection and heart are engaged.

In my quest to show Sande the affection she needs and deserves, I've even had to develop an appreciation for the color mauve. Sande has me watching *Project Runway* with her. It's a TV show where clothes designers go to a store, buy crazy things, and then craft a formal gown from those items. It's hardly typical fare for someone like me who eats, sleeps, and drinks football. But because I love my wife and she's fascinated by the show, I watch it with her . . . as well as *Top Chef.* Both certainly help me get in touch with my feminine side.

> *Sex is not centered on a woman's vagina. It begins in her heart.*

## Communication

The second top need for a woman is communication. Women are relational by nature; they love to share. Men, can you imagine saying to a buddy, "Hey, Tom, want to stop at that little restaurant there and share a tuna salad sandwich? Maybe we could split a salad too." Never in a million years would you hear such a statement from a man. But women? Not only do they share their experiences, they relive every detail and nuance about what he said and she said. I'm always amazed at the length of time my wife can talk on the phone with our daughters. She asks questions I wouldn't even think to ask.

When a friend of one of our daughters got engaged, I just wanted to know how long she'd known the guy and when the wedding was. Sande grabbed the phone from me and cooed, "Oh, isn't that precious? So tell me . . ." And they were off and running about how, where, and when exactly the guy proposed, specifics about what the diamond looked like, what colors the bride was considering for the wedding, what the guy's family was like, and on and on. I shook my head and laughed. Men and women couldn't be any more different. But I have to admit, hearing all the goings-on *was* entertaining. If it were up to us men, the conversation would have lasted about 10 seconds.

*Not only do women share their experiences, they relive every detail and nuance about what he said and she said.*

However, over the years of our marriage, I've learned that listening is one of the top skills a husband needs to learn. If I love and care about my wife—and I do—I will listen to anything and everything she has to say. In the flow of conversation, I'll ask appropriate questions to show that I'm engaged and that I care. By actively listening, I'm saying, "Honey, I care about you, and I'm interested in what both excites and concerns you. I want to spend time with you. I want to know what's important to you."

That means when I walk in the door, I don't talk first about my day. I ask her, "How was your day, sweetheart?" I find out what's pressing on her mind, her heart, her schedule.

When you do that, your wife thinks, *Wow, what a man. I know he's had a very busy day himself, but he really cares what I'm up against. I can talk to him about anything. We're in this together.*

### Commitment

All women can relate to hectic days. When I was doing a presentation in Canada on stress in a woman's life, one woman asked a question about how to get kids to do homework. She added that she was homeschooling six kids right now.

Talk about a huge job—teacher, mother, and disciplinarian, all rolled up into one. Is it any wonder she's tired?

Some women have the ankle-biter battalion circling their mommy wagon all day. Others juggle kids at home and full-time or part-time work outside the home, with constant demands from both directions. Still others put out one fire in the workplace just as another is ignited, causing them to feel like they can't accomplish enough either at home or at work.

When men don't get their work done for the day, they shrug and say, "Well, I did what I could. There's always tomorrow." A woman? She is wracked with guilt for not being able to do it all, has difficulty saying no because she doesn't want to disappoint people, and will often push herself far beyond her limits to try to get more done than is humanly possible. Why else in a lot of homes do you see the husband channel-surfing late in the evening while the wife is still doing the dishes, lining up her to-do list for the next day, finishing laundry, and simultaneously helping her child memorize the table of elements for his chemistry test?

I call those wives "Velcro women" because everything sticks to them. They are the ones who keep the family moving in multiple directions. Think about it. Who remembers that your four-year-old has a dance recital on Tuesday? Runs the kids to and from school and packs their lunches? Goes grocery shopping over lunch? Does dishes and laundry in stages as she runs in and out of the house completing projects? Talks your junior higher through her latest crush? Helps your fifth grader who's wrestling with math? Provides the chocolate chip cookies for your work lunch? Accompanies you to that colleague banquet? And still manages to hold down a part-time or full-time job outside the home? Your wife, that's who. Is it any wonder she's tired by the end of the day and too pooped to whoop?

> *For a woman, foreplay is all about commitment. It's about having a strong man who jumps in when she needs help.*

But what if in the middle of her hectic day she received a text from her husband that said, "Honey, I just wanted you to know how much I love you. Is there anything I can pick up for you after work today?"

What is that husband doing? He's showing his commitment to her best interests and to his family by offering to help. You see, for a woman, foreplay is all about commitment. It's about having a strong man who jumps in when she needs help. The kind of man who wipes off sticky countertops, makes breakfast every Saturday and Sunday morning, gets up three times a night with the toddler who has the flu, and volunteers to pick up the kids from school because he got off work early. What does that tell his wife? *I care about you and the kids, and our family is my first priority.*

Gentlemen, whenever you say, "Honey, what can I do to help?" you're making love to your wife.

## What Stops a Woman from Wanting Sex

I have a wife and four daughters. I was reared with an older sister. As a psychologist, I spend my days talking with women from across the world about parenting, marriage, and family topics. So even though I'm a man, I know women pretty well.

Women in general are warm and relational. They love closeness. They will hug anything that moves—including other women, children, the neighbor's cat that strays onto their porch, and anyone who is having a rough go of it in life. So why is it that, when it comes to the act of sex—the ultimate relational closeness—the majority of women would rather scrub floors? What are we men doing wrong? Or what are we not doing? And what do the excuses really mean?

*She doesn't like being vulnerable.*

None of us likes to be vulnerable. And in marriage, there's an intense vulnerability in submitting to and pleasing each other in sex. It takes couples back to when Adam and Eve were naked and unashamed in that beautiful garden. They didn't even notice they were naked; it was a normal part of their existence. But when their eyes were opened after they ate from the one tree God said not to eat from, they scrambled to find fig leaves to cover themselves. Women have been scrambling to cover themselves ever since. Is it any surprise, then, that when women do enjoy sex, they like the lights dimmed?

Sex is the most intimate act you can engage in with someone else. But it can also be one of the most distant ones. It can be perfunctory, void of emotion or passion or communication. If you ask most couples, they don't talk during sex, and that is a huge detriment, especially to a relational woman who is high on communication.

But a man who compliments his bride, who whispers to her how desirable she is as he touches her, will stir new heights of passion.

*She distrusts or dislikes intimacy due to past experiences.*

Women may be uncomfortable with sexual intimacy or even fear it for many reasons.

Those who grew up in conservative homes may have developed a view that sex is dirty. For example, when Diane began developing physically, her father pulled back from her. He rarely hugged her anymore, and when he did, it was awkward. She now had breasts, and he didn't know how to deal with those changes. Diane interpreted her father's actions as, *You're not beautiful enough to be loved.* All at a time when she was wondering how other males would view her as a young woman. She struggled greatly with her self-image during her teen years. She constantly dieted, worrying that she was too fat to be pretty. Desperate for male attention, she flaunted her development to lure in guys. Eventually she fell into the trap of bulimia.

Other women have been sexually abused by a trusted family member, date-raped, or abused by an ex. If you have undergone such trauma, you will understandably struggle with trust. The people you expected to protect you were the ones who abused you. Early sex can change a woman's view of herself and make her believe she is unworthy of love and affection.

> *Early sex can change a woman's view of herself and make her believe she is unworthy of love and affection.*

But that's a lie. Every woman is a unique creature, created by God Almighty, and deserves love and affection. Women who have undergone abuse need committed, understanding men who will be gentle with them and ask about their needs and fears. If this is one of the issues you face together in your marriage, a few sessions with a trusted counselor might be beneficial.

*She doesn't feel appreciated by her man.*

Every day a woman is saying to her man, "Do you really love me? Do you really care?" How does she measure that love? It doesn't start in the bedroom. In fact, if that's the only place her husband seems to show affection—to get sex—that turns her off. She will feel demeaned and disrespected.

A woman can come from a difficult background, where she was unloved and abused, and still be an eager sexual partner in her marriage bed. But the reason has everything to do with the way her husband treats her. If his attitude is, "Are you gonna put out tonight or not?" he won't win her trust and confidence or capture her heart. He'll get an accommodating wife at best, but never an eager one. She'll grow more bitter and resentful toward him every time they have sex.

What warms a woman up? When a man picks up his clothes and hangs them up, folds laundry, arranges dates, helps with the kids, listens to his wife talk about her concerns, and kisses her when he leaves the house and walks in the door, she will naturally respond eagerly to marital intimacy. After all, she has a man who is enthralled with her beauty, desires her, wants to bring her pleasure, and shows his understanding and appreciation of what she does every day by helping out

*Every day a woman is saying to her man, "Do you really love me? Do you really care?"*

wherever he can. Now that's a winning combo that will steal any woman's heart and make it yours forever, gentlemen.

### She's continually multitasking.

I don't know a woman in the world who can think romance and sex if there are dishes in her kitchen sink. She may be fulfilling the desires of her in-the-mood husband, but her brain? It's on the dishes. *I just did them this morning. Then I did them after dinner again. So how, in the space of two hours, can the sink be entirely full of dishes again?*

That's because women, unlike men, are multitasking creatures. At lunchtime, men simply eat lunch. When women eat lunch, they accomplish other things: making a grocery list, switching the laundry or zipping off to the dry cleaner's, making dentist appointments for the kids, scheduling the dog's toenail clipping, and running a sack lunch a kid forgot to school. It's no wonder that a woman's brain has difficulty shutting off the flow of to-dos to focus on sex, even as much as she loves her man.

Women don't need bigger houses, more expensive cars, more clothing. What they need is an actively involved man who is committed to helping out and taking some of those items off her list for the day. Gentlemen, if you don't think your wife accomplishes 17 items in the time you accomplish one, just step into her shoes for the day. Ask her to hand over her list of items, and then do exactly what she'd do for 24 hours. I guarantee at the end of that 24 hours you'll be draped, nearly lifeless, over your La-Z-Boy.

So it's important that when you arrive home, you haven't expended all your energy or your word count for the day. You're needed at home—by your wife, by your family—to help out, to listen, to be at the dinner table, and to do whatever needs to be done afterward.

When I was growing up, I always thought my mother was like an owl. She could swivel her head and see anything I was up to, which was usually a lot.

> *I don't know a woman in the world who can think romance and sex if there are dishes in her kitchen sink.*

That multitasking nature is also why my beloved wife can't have sex if anyone is within five miles of our home. Believe me, we tried. When our kids were young, we'd let them watch cartoons on Saturday mornings, just so Mommy and Daddy could "talk." However, it would only be minutes before at least two of them were at our locked bedroom door.

"Daddy? Are you in there? I can't hear you talking. I thought you said you and Mommy needed to talk," Krissy would say.

"Get away from that door!" I'd yell in a fatherly tone.

Sande would raise an imperious eyebrow. "You're a psychologist, and that's the best you can do?"

The tiny feet would scamper away, but then they'd be back seconds later. One time at the worst possible moment, right when I was circling the planet Jupiter with my bride, I heard little Krissy say, "Kevey, I think they need our help. You better go get the hammer so we can get the door open."

Yes, the enemy is small. And they can wreak havoc on your sex life. Mama Bear will always have her ears tuned to the least little whimper from one of her cubs, whereas Papa Bear hears them but has his eyes on his hunting mission.

That's why couples have to get really good at being creative.

*She's bored—the glow is missing.*

Men like predictability; women like variety. Men, if you wonder whether that's true, just go take a look at your closet. Stare at her side. She might have 20 pairs of shoes. Then go stare at your side. You might have three or four. Women don't wear the same clothes two days in a row. We men? We give that shirt the sniff test, and if it's not too rank, back on it goes.

A woman likes variety; she's bored with routine. Just because she's turned on by a certain touch one time doesn't mean she'll be turned on by that same act the next time. But men want the road map to the destination. They try to follow the same route they did the previous time . . . and end up boring their bride.

You see, one night she may be up for a quickie. But two days later, she wants slow, languid sex with lots of foreplay. A male's job? To figure out what kind of mood his wife is in.

> *Sex, to a woman, isn't a onetime event. It's an all-day affair. It begins with how her man treats her from the instant he sees her in the morning.*

Some men think foreplay is taking a shower, then exiting to do their best *Dancing with the Stars* audition. As Sandra once said to me, "Uh, that's not a good dance."

My feelings were hurt, but I understood.

Sex, to a woman, isn't a onetime event. It's an all-day affair. It begins with how her man treats her from the instant he sees her in the morning.

Sex is an amazing marital glue. Without it, a woman doesn't receive the affection, communication, and commitment she craves, and a man's needs aren't fulfilled either. Then that couple grows distant. Discontent often seethes beneath the surface. Both husband and wife feel emotionally empty and bury themselves in their work and/or in the children.

What you deserve is the kind of sex that's intensely exciting—where you can't keep your hands off each other. Do you remember those times early in your relationship that the world seemed to disappear when you made love, lost in each other's embrace? If that intensity has cooled, and sex isn't as eager, fun, and adventurous as it used to be, it's time to get back on track—back to thrilling sex.

When sex is satisfying for both parties and you desire each other's bodies, you won't be embarrassed by any extra pounds or jiggles. You'll make the best use of those love handles. For those of you who don't like your work and are only putting in the hours to bring home the bacon, sex with the one you love can make life worth living. And for those who are with toddlers all day, a husband who lights a candle, dances with you around the bedroom, and tells you how wonderful you are is a romantic adventure that will keep you going amid the Pampers changes and juice spills.

If you want to have more sex and better sex as a couple, a husband needs to sensitively understand and address his wife's vulnerability, her background, the way she's treated, and her multi-tasking nature, and think variety. To have a sexually fulfilling relationship requires more than a physical jumping in the sack together. It means each of you truly knows the other.

## Top Four "Dos" for Men to Get That Female Slow Cooker Simmering

Men are streamlined, easy. They're ready to go anytime, anywhere. Women are more complicated. I often compare men to microwaves and women to slow cookers. She may be slower to warm up, but when she does, oh, the incredible flavors you'll enjoy together. So, gentlemen, this section is especially for you, since we males often need some suggestions to get our own wheels turning. If you want to warm up that slow cooker, here are four "dos" to pay attention to.

*Let your wife be a woman, and show your appreciation.*

Let me point out the obvious. Your wife is a woman. She's not a man. She thinks differently than you, talks differently than you (in fact, she can talk circles around you), and responds differently than you to the same situation. Does that make your relationship predictable and easy? No, but it'll never be boring either.

Some of you are saying, "Amen! You can say that again."

Well, good, I got your attention. Now, see if you can hang on for the rest of this section, even if it's in the middle of Monday Night Football. See what I mean about men being singly focused?

What if your bride asked in the middle of that game, "Richard, do you really love me? Lately, you haven't . . ."?

The shortsighted man might wave her off and say, "Uh, honey, it's almost the end of the second quarter. Can we talk about this at halftime?"

But the smart husband who's focused on a long-term, satisfying relationship would do something else. He'd mute the television, set the remote control down, and turn his whole body toward her. Looking her directly in the eye, he'd say kindly, "Sweetheart, is there something you want to tell me?"

That's the man who will reap entertainment in the bedroom that's far more scintillating than sitting in an armchair watching football.

You married that woman because you were attracted to her differences, including the fact that she cared enough to ask you questions about yourself and your day, so let her be different. Allow her to be the communications expert she naturally is. Yes, she may be fussy about details and sometimes have bad timing—like in the middle of the football game—but that fussiness and commitment to improving your relationship make her who she is. It's a part of that mystique you fell in love with in the first place. After all, marrying someone just like you wouldn't be very exciting, would it?

So why not let your differences work for you as a couple rather than against you? Men enjoy sex the most but women enjoy snuggling the most. Men talk in grunts but women need words, sentences, and even full paragraphs. Men crave respect for the hard work they do. They show their commitment to their family by working hard to bring home the bacon, while a woman's definition of commitment to family is more along the lines of "being there." Is it any wonder, then, that women who play two roles—bringing home the bacon and frying it up in the pan—feel additionally stressed? Although they're carrying a full-time or part-time workload outside the home and still carrying their regular workload at home, they continually feel guilt for not "being there" for their kids and husband as much as they'd like.

> *Marrying someone just like you wouldn't be very exciting, would it?*

Men have to accept a woman's top needs—for affection, communication, and commitment—and learn how to read her. The prevailing winds of a woman change every day, and even from hour to hour. A man who can adjust to those changes, approach her sensitively, meet her needs, and ensure she feels loved creates the environment of warmth a woman craves.

In short, let her be a woman. Take her out for a nice dinner. You might even break down and go to a salad buffet every once in a while, since she loves variety. Show your appreciation of her femininity when she dresses up for you. Whistle at her and touch those curves, showing that you still desire her. Make her an appointment for a haircut or a facial as a surprise, and don't wince when you see the bill. Smile and compliment her on how beautiful she looks.

Encouraging your woman to be a female doesn't make you a wuss. In fact, it makes you even more of a man. You can still wear the same shirt and ball cap you've worn for three days. You can eat the same breakfast two weeks in a row. You don't have to eat quiche for lunch just because she does. You can still burp and release other gaseous noises . . . but please, not in her presence. And before you get amorous, brush your teeth and take a shower. Add a dash of cologne to tickle her oh-so-female nose. Then take that woman in your arms and start telling her what you appreciate about her.

Bet you anything the juices in that slow cooker will be boiling before long.

*Listen, but don't problem-solve unless she asks.*

When we men talk, most of the time we exchange information so we can solve problems. We're goal-oriented and short-winded with our conversation.

When your wife talks, she isn't necessarily giving you that information to go from point A to point B. She is talking because she is in the midst of processing some information or an emotion and wants to share that with you. She isn't necessarily looking for you to solve that problem for her; she simply wants you to be a listening ear. Much of the time, she will already have decided what she needs to do, but she longs for you—strong, wise man that you are—to empathize with her, relate to her, and say, "Honey, I know you'll do the right thing. You always do. I believe in you."

That something she's telling you may or may not seem important to you, but you should treat it as important. When she talks, you need to actively listen. Listening in between commercials or with a grunt won't satisfy her need for conversation. It would

> *Listening in between commercials or with a grunt won't satisfy her need for conversation. It would be like you taking one bite of a perfectly done steak and then having the waiter whisk it away from you.*

be like you taking one bite of a perfectly done steak and then having the waiter whisk it away from you.

Yes, she will give you far more details than you want to know. You like the CliffsNotes; she wants to tell you the whole novel. But you can't capture your wife's heart unless you are engaged in her world.

Little things matter to women—texts to tell her you're thinking of her; a quick phone call in the midst of your business trip; a surprise flower just to say "I love you"; a midnight run to pick up Pepto-Bismol. Your wife is continually watching you, absorbing what you say, your expressions, and how you listen to and respond to her requests. Your involvement and your interest in the little and big things of her day make all the difference in the health of your marriage.

*Be her rock.*

Let's face it. From day one of our existence, we males are primed to compete—to be tough. Sure, we may be little boys inside, wanting to please our women, but on the outside we want to be seen as boulders.

Well, your wife wants that too. She wants you to be the strength she can count on, that immovable force who will protect her and your family against anything, whether it's the neighbor who's angry because your son trampled his flower bushes, a mouse that has taken up residence in your cereal cabinet, or an ex who keeps showing up uninvited.

I can't think of a single woman I've counseled over the past four decades who said, "You know, Dr. Leman, I want a guy I can push

50

around easily, a guy I can control, a guy who's a limp noodle, who just does what I want him to do and has no mind of his own." No, women admire, need, and respect our male strength if it is used in the proper way—to support, encourage family members, and provide a solid, safe foundation for our home.

Because women are wired innately to be relational, they also care intensely about relationships. Along with that caring comes deep emotion, which sometimes leaks out in a form we men dread— tears. Most men don't know what to do with them. Many of us tend to edge into another room, either saying nothing or muttering, "Uh, honey, when you're done with that, maybe we could do dinner."

But the "rock" man, when he sees tears, gathers his wife in his strong arms, lets her cry it out, and simply holds her until she's ready to talk about it.

*Women admire, need, and respect our male strength if it is used in the proper way—to support, encourage family members, and provide a solid, safe foundation for our home.*

I guarantee, gentlemen, that if you do that, it doesn't matter whether you're only five feet eight inches and 140 pounds. You'll be bigger to her than Dwayne Johnson, The Rock.

*Get active—both inside and outside the bedroom.*

Funny thing, I spend most of my counseling time helping women get active in the bedroom and helping men get active elsewhere.

If a man only makes love to his wife in the bedroom, both are missing out. He needs to make love to her outside the bedroom. No, I'm not talking about switching rooms where they have sex (though that is nice too). I'm talking about helping.

A man who carries groceries in for his wife or, even better, shops for her on his way home or on his day off is extending a romantic gesture that says, "I care about you and about us. I want to make your day easier." He's the same kind of man who calls her when she's driving in a rainstorm to see if she's all right, making her feel well cared for, cherished, and protected. He's the type of man who helps their kids with homework and tucks them into bed and is a supportive, loving, involved daddy. When he does those things, he's making love to his wife. She thinks, *Wow, out of all the people on the planet, I'm the one who was lucky enough to marry that man.*

Think of it this way, men. Every time you carry the laundry up the stairs for your wife, every time you take out the garbage or vacuum the hallway, every time you bring milk home from the store, you are gaining points of respect with your wife. You are saying, "I'm a man who can be counted on to help out with whatever you need."

A woman whose husband serves her practically is going to be a much more willing participant in their bed, because she appreciates his efforts and respects him as a man. Sure, she looks capable, juggling all those tasks. But that doesn't mean she wouldn't welcome her husband's help or that she doesn't need it. Nothing would please her more than to have you ride in on your white steed to rescue her from a difficult situation, to spirit her away for a break, or simply to help get the job done.

> *I spend most of my counseling time helping women get active in the bedroom and helping men get active elsewhere.*

A woman who has a good sex life tends to experience less stress in life. She knows she's in good hands with her husband, because he has her best in mind. That's why he doesn't mind changing diapers, cleaning up vomit, or spraying the hornets' nest in the mailbox. That man is willing to do anything for his wife. In response, he gains a partner who is willing to do anything with, and for, him.

### Great Ways to Woo Your Wife

Want to show your woman how much you love her? Then try these simple ideas—or combine one or more into a getaway evening or weekend! Every time you brainstorm something special to do for her, plan it, and carry out the steps, you deposit dividends in your wife's affection bank.

*Arrange a surprise dinner out, complete with a babysitter.*

Call Grandma, your wife's best girlfriend, or a qualified babysitter and make arrangements for her to come to the house at least an hour before you arrive home. Let your wife know you are taking her out for dinner and have made all the arrangements necessary for the kids. That hour before you arrive will give her time to get things squared away with the babysitter and time to prepare herself. We men need little preparation. All we have to do is go potty, brush our teeth, and loosen our tie (or put one on), and we're ready to go. Women need advance notice—time to shower, fix their hair, put on makeup, and try on some different outfits in their wardrobe to find the perfect one.

*Hire some cleaning help.*

Hire Merry Maids or some other local cleaning staff to come in and clean the entire house. From firsthand experience, I know that four Merry Maids can do it in an hour . . . even while you're at dinner. That way, when your wife walks in the door after that romantic dinner, she won't have heaps of dishes to do or brownie crumbs to clean up from the couch. She'll have that satisfied "wow, look at that, everything is clean" feeling.

*Romance her.*

Prearrange with the restaurant and waiter for them to hand-deliver a favorite flower, a little gift or two, and some love notes that you've already dropped off. Along with the appetizer or salad, the waiter shows up with your wife's favorite flower and a note you've handwritten: *One of the reasons I love you so much is . . .*

During the main entrée, the waiter brings a second flower, or a little gift if you prefer, with another handwritten love note: *Another reason I love you is . . .*

And during dessert, that waiter brings a third flower or gift with another handwritten note: *I'm so glad I married you, and I'd do it all over again in an instant.*

The glow in her eyes will be worth all your work.

*Make dinner for her.*

Your wife may be a gourmet cook, but she'll happily eat anything you make if you suggest, "Honey, let me handle dinner tonight while you relax a little." Even better, draw a bath for her before you start cooking. Add a fragrance she likes to the water. Place a candle nearby for an extra romantic touch. Add a couple fluffy towels and a robe to the setting. There's no woman alive who wouldn't sigh walking into that bathroom, knowing she has a guy who appreciates her. No matter what the dinner tastes like, she'll give you five stars for effort.

If you have children, give a qualified babysitter money to take those kids to the Cheese Breath Rodent Place, with another $20 for lots of game tokens to keep them occupied.

If you're like many men, you might cringe at these suggestions. *That sounds like a lot of work. I'm not very good at planning ahead. Is this something I have to do every five years, or more regular than that?*

You do it a lot more regular than that, Rocky. Consider this. Every day your wife's head spins with to-dos, and many of those have to do with keeping your world spinning on its axis too. The least you can do is take some time out to focus on her and what she enjoys.

There are days when your Velcro woman wonders, *Is all this worth it? I'm tired beyond belief. Being a mom and a wife seems to be such a thankless job. Nobody seems to notice.* But if you shower affection on your wife in practical ways that show your support of her as well as your admiration of her and her femininity, she will look at you and think, *Well, others may not notice, but he notices. What a lucky woman I am!*

Your Velcro woman also needs time away from the kids, where she doesn't have to worry about them. Moms always worry about their cubs. If their cubs are not in her den, she worries all the more. That's why it's important you make sure someone very capable is taking care of your cubs. If you allay her fears, she can thoroughly enjoy time with you.

Do any of these things, use your imagination to think up more, and you'll be reaching into your wife's heart big-time and meeting her top three needs for affection, communication, and commitment.

## Let the Chandelier Shake . . .

Over the years, as I've met women across the country, I've asked them what their top three stressors are. The order may vary, but it's always the same three: lack of time, kids, and husband. Here's what's interesting—even those who work outside the home didn't mention work. That's because the things closest to a woman's heart are her relationships at home. When I asked the women to clarify what they meant by lack of time, it always came down to the fact that they wanted to spend more time with the people they love.

Well, guess who is in the best position to help with all three of a woman's top stressors? Her husband! Problem is, most of you women look so capable at juggling tasks that we men often assume you're handling everything just fine and don't need our help. And being the tenderhearted boys we are, we don't want to offer assistance and then get slapped down. We want to please you; we simply don't know where to start. So kindly offer some suggestions both inside and outside the bedroom, and watch us go to town.

Say, "Honey, I need some time to myself. Just a couple of hours. Can you watch the kids after you get settled in from work tonight?"

Your husband's chest will puff out like a rooster's, happy to please his bride, and he'll even hurry home from work to pluck your five-year-old son off the dining room chandelier he's swinging from.

Say, "Honey, I'd like to try something different tonight." Touch him intimately, whisper the suggestion in his ear, or move his hand to a specific location, and he will most eagerly oblige.

He might even shake the chandelier and do a little swinging from it himself to make his own Tarzan and Jane love story.

# *Tuesday*

## Why Men Want Sex

What men need the most, what they want the most, and
why they need foreplay just as much as women do.

There's a reason guys have so many names for their penis—it's
been their favorite body part from the time they were young
boys. In fact, healthy men think about sex at least 33 times a day!

If you're a guy, you're nodding at that statement. *You got that
right!*

If you're a woman, you're thinking something far different. *Are
you kidding me? That's disgusting! Don't men think about other
things? I barely have time to take a shower before the next thing
on my to-do list hits me. No wonder my husband hasn't been able
to fix the porch step for five years.*

But you see, thinking about sex 33 times a day is natural for
men. We're wired to think about it. And it's not perverted at all if
thinking about sex drives that man of yours into your arms time
and time again. Or if it makes him floor the accelerator of his car
so he can beat you home to set up a romantic environment he
knows you'll love.

When you understand what men need and want and how you can fulfill those needs, you'll have a guy who not only will make it his mission to pleasure you in the bedroom but also will clean up the kids' vomit, fix whatever is broken in the house, and make a late-night run to the grocery store just because you're craving chocolate. Talk about a win-win for both of you! A little knowledge goes a long way with men.

## Getting into Your Man's Brain

Have you ever wished, even for a minute, you could get into your husband's brain? To know what he's thinking? To experience what he's feeling? Here's a little peek.

### Attracted to the physical

Have you ever seen a squirrel that's lured and distracted by a shiny piece of metal that flashes in the sunlight? That critter can't resist creeping closer to check out the object. Men are like that—they're attracted to shiny pieces of metal that flash in the sunlight, especially if that blingy metal is in the alluring shape of a female. Then that male squirrel tries his best to draw the female's attention by slapping the bark of a tree with his paw and wildly flicking that bushy tail. If you walked into your local high school and observed the young men trying to attract their female classmates, you'd see a lot of similarities in behavior.

Men are attracted to the physical. They are always looking around them. They have wildly different attention spans than females. They are drawn to scope out certain details, such as how computer gamers' push for better graphics sparked huge changes in the entire technology industry, how the front end was adapted on the newest Cadillac, and how snugly the uniform fits the waitress serving his dinner. Men look at objects and people for a much shorter time than women do, but they are more active in their attention. They don't simply gaze; they evaluate all aspects.

Sure, it might drive wives a bit crazy, especially when that husband is checking out a woman other than her, but there's good news too.

Look at it this way, ladies. When your husband first saw you, he didn't merely give you a passing glance. He checked you out head to toe, found you fascinating, and decided you were worth investing time in. He relentlessly pursued his purpose of getting you to go out with him on a date.

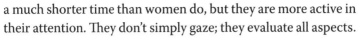

*Have you ever seen a squirrel that's lured and distracted by a shiny piece of metal that flashes in the sunlight?*

When you met that man of yours, you checked him out head to toe too. You noticed he was neatly dressed, was clean, and had good manners. But you were more interested in gazing into his eyes, hearing his stories about growing up with his siblings, learning what he does in his free time, and watching his body language for signals of what he was really thinking about you. That's because women are attracted to the relational.

Reminisce about your first date. Who did most of the talking? Chances are, it was you. You were doing what you do best—relating. You were pulling together all the angles of this potential relationship that stirred your heart with romantic feelings and your mind with the possibilities of what might happen. Afterward you relived every bit of this exciting beginning of interest with your best girlfriends. If you're like most women, you called one girlfriend and told the story. Then you called another girlfriend and told the story, in even more detail, all over again.

Meanwhile, that guy you were gushing over was doing what men do best—appreciating all your best features in his recall and brainstorming how to go after the prize.

And evidently his plan worked, since you married him.

*Born to compete*

Any male who is healthy psychologically has a built-in drive to go after what he wants. Once your husband focuses on a goal or project, it isn't easy to sidetrack him. He goes after it with determination. That's because males instinctively want to be number one.

When you're driving on the highway or expressway sometime, take a look at who is driving in the fast lane. Do your own mini survey. Stay in the right-hand lane for 10 minutes and see who flies by you. The majority of the time it's the male drivers—especially younger male drivers—who hustle by. The insurance companies aren't dumb. Young males are more prone to driving faster and taking risks, so it's no wonder their car insurance is higher.

> *Any male who is healthy psychologically has a built-in drive to go after what he wants.*

We males are primed to compete. Nobody is going to zoom around and ahead of us without having to work really hard at it. When I drive, I check out the traffic patterns and change lanes frequently to see how far ahead I can get. If my beloved bride were driving, it would take us twice as long to get somewhere because she'd be toodling in the right-hand lane, smelling the roses along the expressway. Me? I'm a man on a mission, trying to get from point A to point B.

Enough said.

*A craving for adventure*

Within the heart of every man is an adventurer. Men like to be on the move, accomplishing the next step to their goal. If you don't believe me, go watch the male species on a playground. Boys are a blur of action, competing for the prize and seeking the thrill of adventure. Some of their contests may seem downright laughable or shocking to girls: Who can hang from the monkey bars with his feet the longest? Who can spin the tire swing the most times without upchucking? Who can spit the farthest? And (after making sure no one else is watching) who can spray an X on a tree with his urine?

The girls? They're off in a little cluster, relating heart to heart, holding hands, and talking about their someday dreams. They're rolling their eyes at the boys' misadventures and saying things like, "Eww, sick. *Boys.*"

That same craving for adventure affects your grown-up boy too. That's why many men, after saying "I do" and enjoying every bit of their honeymoon, think, *Well, I can check the marriage job off my list. Secured my woman. And boy, is she a great one. I'm a lucky guy. Now, let's see . . . what's next on my list of things to do?* And they're off to conquer the next mountain, patting themselves on the back for doing the marriage job well.

Meanwhile, the bride, upon her return from the honeymoon, is thinking, *Finally, time with my guy 24/7. I can hold his hand anytime I want, and we can snuggle all weekend. We can talk about our days over dinner, lingering as long as we want, until the candles run out.* . . . A romantic sigh. *It's so nice to marry my best friend.*

Imagine that bride's surprise when her groom is happily catapulting on to the next thing and isn't as physically or emotionally present as she'd like. She feels deflated, even unloved, and wonders what happened to her tender, romantic husband. The groom? He's clueless as to why his bride seems touchy all of a sudden and down in the dumps. He's assuming that all is good now at home because he's won his prize—the woman he loves. But that woman is still all about relating, and she needs his warmth and affection on a continual basis.

No wonder the two sometimes clash.

---

**Real Men Talk**
*What I Love about My Wife*

- She supports me in my decisions and shows appreciation for the work I do.
- Even when I mess up, she loves me.
- She shares my interests—or at least acts interested (ha).
- She makes me feel invincible, like Superman . . . like I can do anything.
- She loves me even when I forget and do little things she hates, like leaving the toilet seat up and squeezing the toothpaste from the middle.
- She listens when I talk. She stops what she's doing, looks me in the eye, and doesn't do the million other things she usually does simultaneously.
- She gives me the short version of anything important that happened that day when I walk in the door. Then I'm not left in the dark, I have time to process, and later I can ask her to give me more info.
- She took a vacation day from work so we could make love all day on my birthday, when the kids were at school.
- She doesn't make me guess what she wants. She just tells me nicely.
- She doesn't badger me with questions.
- I overheard her on the phone with a friend talking about how "awesome" of a husband I am.
- She bought a new nightie, and it wasn't even our anniversary.

---

## A Man's Top Three Needs

What does a man want the most? To be wanted, needed, and respected—in that order.

### Want me

Your guy may be 45, balding, and a little paunchy around the middle, but he needs to know that you still desire him. If you make him feel like a king in the bedroom, there's nothing that man won't go after and accomplish. He might hate the job he goes to every day, but he'll continue to go because he's doing it for you.

It's easy for most guys to become sexually excited. Just leave off your bra, and one peek at your contours will gain his attention. Or simply brush the fly of his pants with your little finger.

Here's the catch, though. His timing may not always be the best in the world, especially if you're in the middle of a project. As a multitasking woman, you've got a lot on your mind. He's got one thing on his mind . . . sex, with you. It's the way you both are wired.

> *If you make him feel like a king in the bedroom, there's nothing that man won't go after and accomplish.*

But consider this: *you* are the only person in the universe who can fulfill what your husband wants right at this moment. The dust bunnies under your couch can wait. It won't matter if you have leftover spaghetti for tomorrow's breakfast (the kids would probably love that anyway) because you don't have time to go grocery shopping. The half hour extra you're doing on that work project won't reap the lifetime dividend you'll get by giving your husband some skin-to-skin time.

One of the most common fights between couples is about sexual frequency. How often should you have sex? The answer will vary from couple to couple. But here's the simple answer: if one of you is longing for sex with your spouse, then the other should be willing to fulfill that need. Doing so is part of developing a healthy marriage by putting the other person first.

Think he can wait? If he has sex on his mind and you shut him down because you're too busy, what does that say to him? "You're not important to me, and I don't find you attractive anymore." The best way to affair-proof your marriage is to treat your husband as both important and attractive. He needs to feel wanted, needed, and fulfilled, or he will be emotionally vulnerable to another person who offers to meet those needs.

However, there will be times when you have something to do that can't wait. That's when you, a female superior in word skills, use your natural language ability to deliver something that's almost as good as the real thing or can heighten it. It's called *anticipation*, and it's a powerful draw.

Let's say you're scrambling to get ready in the morning because you have a big presentation at work. You're standing in the bathroom when your husband presses against you from behind, then reaches around to caress your breast. There's no mistaking his intent.

You've got some choices.

Choice #1: You slap away his hand and say, "Not now! I gotta be at work in half an hour."

The result: You go away annoyed, and he goes away sexually frustrated, thinking you don't understand his needs and consider your work more important than him.

Choice #2: You allow him a few seconds or even a full minute to caress your breast. When he pulls away, you say in a sexy tone, "Hey! You forgot the other one."

The result: There's a big intake of breath, and he reaches around to fondle the other breast. Now that's a rare treat he won't forget. And how long did that take? Just a few seconds of your time, but your man knew you loved his touch and wanted him to come back for more.

Choice #3: You allow him to caress your breasts, then reach around and do some grabbing of your own. You do some quick math: *Okay, if we had a quickie, I could still take a three-second shower and put my hair up in a ponytail for work.*

The result: You and your husband are both smiling and thinking about each other all day.

Choice #4: Because you know your man's number one need is to be wanted, you allow him a few seconds to caress your breast. Then you swivel toward him to give him a full frontal view to feast his eyes on and say, "Wow, you're really in the mood, huh? Unfortunately, I have to be at work in half an hour. But let me tell you something." You lean forward suggestively and put your arms around him. "If you can buzz straight home from work tonight, I'll have an even better and bigger surprise awaiting you than we could manage right now. I promise you'll love it." You deliver a deep kiss that takes his breath away. You whisper in his ear, "And that's just a little taste of what's coming."

The result: You've delivered the gift of anticipation that will guarantee when the clock hits 5:00, he'll be heading your way.

There are times when having sex at that moment works and times when it doesn't. Your tough guy loves to be touched, and Mr. Happy doesn't know anything about schedules. In fact, as soon as that testosterone starts coursing, he forgets everything on the agenda for the day. But when you can't, promising a full workout later—and then following through on that promise—will keep a goofy grin plastered on your husband's face until he sees you again. Instead of only minutes of passion, you'll be giving him an entire *day* of anticipation. And he'll be thinking about you all that time.

> *Mr. Happy doesn't know anything about schedules. In fact, as soon as that testosterone starts coursing, he forgets everything on the agenda for the day.*

Men are wired to always be ready. But that wiring is what draws him back to you time and again—to come home to you, to get physically close to you, to relate to you. Every time you improve your sexual communication, you improve your marital intimacy and relationship overall.

That's a pretty big payoff for a little time in the sack.

### Need me

You're a multitasking woman, spinning lots of plates simultaneously. Your husband watches you do all that, jaw agape. You're a little intimidating because you're so good at that master juggling act. But here's a secret about men you need to know. We want to be your hero. In spite of our manly physique, we're little boys at heart. Mama used to be the most important person in our world—the person we wanted to please most. But since we met and married you, you've become that person who is most important to us. We long to please you, to help you out. However, sometimes we don't know what to do. You look so capable.

When you say, "Oh, no, honey, I've got it. I'll finish up here," you might think you're being kind and giving your husband a break. But if that statement is a common occurrence in your household, what a man hears is, "Okay, now, run along, little boy. I'll take care of it. You'll only mess it up. So why don't you go do something else?"

Men often feel like they're not really needed at home—as if all the family wheels on the wagon will stay turning whether they're home and involved or not. So encourage your man a bit, and he can be a wonderful resource. He may not do things like you do them, or as precisely as you do them, but he'll get the job done. His dinner for the kids may not have all the food groups, but it'll fill their tummies. His idea of giving the baby with the poopy diaper a bath may be to hose her off in the yard, instead of the loving play in the bath time you'd plan.

By the way, yes, I did that once—hosed my daughter off in the backyard—and caught all sorts of grief from my wife when she found out about it later. But I got the job done, the mess was all biodegradable, the baby got clean, and the neighbors got a chuckle to make their day better. What's not to like about all that?

Men love to problem-solve. Want to see us shine? Hand us a problem, and we'll pursue it until we solve it. Your husband wants to be your fix-it man, your go-to guy. Solving problems, in fact, addresses all three of our top needs—to be wanted, needed, and respected. Want some help? Just ask, and we're happy to oblige. Otherwise, you might look like you're doing so well handling things yourself that we wouldn't dare to step in.

> *Men often feel like they're not really needed at home—as if all the family wheels on the wagon will stay turning whether they're home and involved or not.*

However, you might want to steer us in the right direction by clarifying the kind of assistance you need. For example: "I'm not sure how I can get everything done today that's on my list. Could you take a look and see what you think is most important?" Handing him your checklist will accomplish your goal in more ways than one. It will give you a second set of eyes to look at what needs to be done and what could wait, plus it allows your husband to see all the things on your list. If he views what you need to do, it gives him the opportunity to say, "Well, I could help with items 3 and 5 over my lunch hour. Right after work I could do item 12. I could handle item 16 this weekend if you could wait until then."

And look at that—you didn't even have to nag for help! That wonderful husband of yours offered . . . all on his own.

When we men know that we are needed, we're more than happy to step up to the plate.

We're especially happy to help in the lovemaking department. If you aren't feeling fulfilled in the area of foreplay, make some suggestions. "Honey, both of the kids will be gone tomorrow night for different activities. I was thinking maybe we could explore a little . . . you know, under the sheets. I especially like these two suggestions"—you slip a scribbled note in his hand—"and thought we might try them tonight."

You can bet that man will work very hard to solve those "problems." In fact, his brain will be working overtime between now and your tryst to come up with some other ideas too.

### Respect me

As a man, your husband craves respect—respect for the work he does outside and inside the home, and respect for his position as someone who can make good decisions. He longs for you to respect his maleness—his strength, his logic, his ability to have a single-minded focus on a task. Great ways to affirm his masculinity are by saying things such as:

- "Honey, I know things at work are really rough right now. But every day I'm so grateful I married a man who powers through even the tough stuff. Thanks for working so hard to provide for our family."
- "I still remember when we went skating on State Street in Chicago while we were dating. When that guy knocked me over, made fun of me, then skated off laughing, you helped me to my feet, steered me to a bench, then went after him. You made him come and apologize to me. I have no idea what you told him after that, but he looked nervous when he left. I felt so safe, so protected, because I was with you. I still feel that same way 11 years later. It's one of the many ways you make me feel womanly and special."

68

- "Wow, I appreciate your perspective. You see all the sides of an issue and then always come up with one or more solutions. Thanks, hon!"
- "Every day I look forward to seeing you after work. You have no idea how wonderful it is to have you as my partner in life."

Statements like that assure your husband he is firmly entrenched in your heart and in your world. The same goes for when you tell the kids, "Okay, Daddy's home, so hold your questions for me until I have time to talk with him." Then you stop what you're doing and give that husband of yours a real welcome-home hug and kiss—enough to make the kids flee, yelling, "Eeewww, that is so gross!"

But it'll make your man grin from ear to ear because he knows that he's your first priority, your number one.

When you treat your husband with respect, you'll get respect back. Nobody's perfect—you or your husband. Both of you will have bad days. But if you expect the best and treat each other that way, you'll often get the best.

> *When you treat your husband with respect, you'll get respect back.*

Meeting your husband's top three needs is important foreplay for him. When he feels wanted, needed, and respected by you, he'll meet your top three needs for affection, communication, and commitment. Even more, because of the competitive guy he is, he'll work continually to up the ante on himself in those departments.

To have a new sex life by Friday, you both have to be willing to work on it and incorporate the principles of this book. But you won't get anywhere if each of you thinks, *Well, I'll do it if my spouse makes the first move.*

Somebody needs to make the first move. Why not you?

**7 Ideas to Keep Your Man Happy . . . in 5 Minutes or Less**

1. Ask for his opinion.
2. Harness his natural logic and analytical power to solve a problem for you.
3. Say "thank you" for the little things he does.
4. Turn toward him when he talks, and fully listen.
5. Touch him when you need to tell him something.
6. Experiment with quick ways to satisfy him sexually.
7. Let him be your hero.

## What Your Man Wants Most from You

We've already talked about a man's top three needs and how meeting them can increase the sizzle in your relationship. Here are some other secrets you need to know to improve your marital intimacy.

*Secret #1: We want to be your knight in shining armor.*

The dashing knight on the white steed isn't only for romantic movies. As old-fashioned as it sounds, your husband really does want to be that for you. He wants to ride into a hard situation, rescue you, and whisk you off into the sunset. He wants to serve you, protect you, defend you—not only physically but also emotionally. He doesn't want anybody to mess with his wife on his watch.

If you need more romance and affection in your relationship, why not view and treat your husband as a romantic knight? When you affirm his masculinity and his protectiveness, you might be surprised at how knightly your husband will become. He may not be able to produce the white steed in your bedroom, but flowers, candles, and sweet somethings in your ear might be a good trade-off, don't you think?

70

*Secret #2: We want you to enter into sex enthusiastically.*

There's nothing more deflating to a husband's masculine ego than a wife who has sex just because he says he wants it, because she's supposed to do it as a "dutiful wife," or because it's written on a schedule as something they do every Saturday night. Then he feels like simply another item on her checklist. But show your pleasure, participate with gusto, tell him what feels good and where to touch, and your man will feel like the most desirable guy in the world. Your desire will drive him to new experimentation that he might otherwise be reticent to risk. And when you choose to initiate sex, you show that you want him and can't get enough of him. Your words of love and direction reveal your need for him—and only him—and your respect for his masculinity.

Yes, sex matters to men greatly. But what's even more important to us is watching you enjoy what we're doing to you. That's the ultimate rush of sensuality that drives us back for more marital intimacy.

You might be concerned that your thighs are a little thicker than you'd like them to be. Your husband isn't thinking about that. He's thinking, *Wowza, I have this amazing woman all to myself. That was incredible sex. I wonder what I could do to turn her on even more next time.*

Ever seen a male peacock fluff out his tail feathers and let out that shrill, piercing squawk to attract a lady friend? Well, that's what happens psychologically to your husband when you enjoy his lovemaking. He's watching you and thinking, *I did that to her. Yup, it was me.*

Let's face it, though. A woman has cycles in which sex is not on her mind, nor is it comfortable for her. Ditto with times of exhaustion and stress. There are times when Mr. Happy is going to be unhappy. However, the key is showing desire and enthusiasm for the experience, even if that experience can't happen right now. It's also about discovering multiple creative ways you both

71

enjoy to bring sexual satisfaction to each other (more about that in the Friday chapter).

Most men need to hold back their desire for sex a bit; most women need to dial up their desire. That's because men have testosterone continually coursing through their body, whereas women's estrogen levels fluctuate. Figuring out your sexual cycle—how often each of you craves sex—will help you talk about your sexual rhythm. Some are on 48-hour or 72-hour cycles, while others are on weekly cycles. How often you have sex isn't up to someone else; it's up to you. Some couples crave sex four nights a week, while others love snuggling together and having sex once a week, when they can take their time. What's important is that you're both fulfilled and satisfied by your sexual communication.

> *Ever seen a male peacock fluff out his tail feathers and let out that shrill, piercing squawk to attract a lady friend? Well, that's what happens psychologically to your husband when you enjoy his lovemaking.*

*Secret #3: We want time alone with you, the person most important to us, to share our thoughts and feelings.*

We men aren't good at sharing thoughts and feelings. Doing so makes us uncomfortable. Seriously, do you see guys discussing things like this with their friends over a break at work?

"I felt really depressed again when I got up this morning. I don't know what's wrong with me this week."

"Well, it's been gray outside for a long time. Maybe you've got SAD or something."

"SAD?"

72

"You know, seasonal affective disorder. A lot of people feel depressed if they don't get to see the sun." A pause, then, "Maybe you need one of those 'happy lights.'"

"Hey, I've heard of those. Do they really work?"

"Well, my friend Mike . . ." The dialogue continues. "And it improved his sex life too."

"Bet that would make my wife happy. I haven't felt like having sex since summer." A laugh.

"Maybe you need a little beach time—some sun, your toes in the sand, your wife bringing you one of those fruity drinks with the pretty umbrella in it to kick things off . . ."

No guy in his right mind would start or continue such a conversation. He'd simply pour himself a cup of coffee, exchange a nod with the other guy at the coffee machine, and go back to his chair to resume the project he was focused on.

That's why your friendship and his time alone with you are so vital to improving your marital intimacy. That man of yours may rarely talk, but when he does, guess who he wants to talk to? You.

Some of you are saying, "Wow . . . then he barely talks at all."

Now you're on track with what I mean. You've got a bunch of friends you text, call, and go out to coffee with. If your husband is the typical male, he might exchange sports or weather statistics with some guys at the office, but the only real friendship he has, where he exchanges anything resembling feelings and emotions? Well, that's with you. He wants you to be his listening ear and to respectfully support his decisions.

> *That man of yours may rarely talk, but when he does, guess who he wants to talk to? You.*

When there's a boxing match and a break is called, the combatants go to separate corners to take a break, strategize, and regroup. That's their safe place, where the other combatant can't come after them. You are the person your husband most needs and wants in his corner. He craves your acceptance, your companionship, and knowing that he belongs to you. You are your husband's "safe corner."

Sometimes he even wants you to chase him around in that corner. When you pursue knowing more about him and meet his top three needs, including his sexual needs, his sigh of appreciation says more than an entire book's worth of words ever could.

*Secret #4: We want you to read us like a book and provide what we need (even when we don't know what we need).*

Let's say your husband calls you on a Friday night. "I'm finally leaving work," he says. "Do you want me to meet you someplace and we'll get a bite to eat?"

"Oh, honey," you say, "you sound a little down."

He sighs. "Yeah, it's been a rough week. Bad. Today's the worst of them all."

It's a family tradition for you, your husband, and the kids to go out for dinner on Friday night. But you're a smart woman, so you say, "Let's not go out for dinner tonight. Why don't I order a pizza and have it delivered? We can relax and have a quiet evening at home."

There's an even bigger sigh on the other end of the phone. "Pizza sounds great. I'm shot. See you in about half an hour."

You get off the phone and think, *Mmm, pizza. Okay then.* You call Grandma, who lives close by. "Mom, you've been talking about taking the kids for a night. Would you be up for taking them tonight? I could have them ready for pickup in 10 minutes."

"I'd love to," Grandma says enthusiastically. "We could go see that new movie they've been talking about."

You order a large pizza with all your husband's favorite toppings while simultaneously getting the kids ready to head out the door. Twelve minutes later, they're gone. You dash into the shower, then put on your favorite perfume and his favorite nightie. (Your favorite nightie is made of flannel; his is made of . . . well, something else.) You throw on a robe to receive the pizza delivery.

When your husband enters the kitchen, you're standing there in your negligee, pizza box in hand like a master waiter. You say seductively, "I'm going to make this really simple for you. The kids are gone for the night. Would you rather enjoy pizza first . . . or enjoy me?"

Notice how fast the pizza box gets tossed to the side.

That's why we have microwaves.

A smart woman learns how to read her husband. Most of us men don't say a lot. We don't naturally share our feelings very quickly. But when you learn to read us, and you pull off surprises like this, you'll have a happy, relieved, thankful, would-knock-down-a-wall-for-you husband on your hands. There's nothing better to relieve stress than a good romp in the hay with the one you love.

So let that man of yours be a male. Allow him to problem-solve, conquer, and be your knight in shining armor. Use that thrill-seeking spark that's been there since boyhood to your best advantage—to launch a few adventures of your own.

Who knows? You might even do a few laps around the moon before you come back to earth.

Now wouldn't that be fun?

# *Wednesday*

## *Someone's in Bed with You . . .*

And it's not only your spouse. How to identify the intruders and reclaim the space for the two of you.

You may think you're having sex with just your spouse. But there are more than the two of you doing the mattress mambo. There are some things that never get unearthed in the average marriage that should be unearthed. But I don't want you to have an average marriage, and neither do you. The average marriage lasts seven years, and both parties walk away with a lot of hurt.

You're reading this book because you want the kind of marital intimacy and heart connection that draws you back together again and again. This chapter will help you identify who the intruders in your bedroom are so you can reclaim the space for the two of you.

On your wedding day, each of you carried a special book up the aisle . . . and then back down the aisle after you were pronounced husband and wife. You didn't leave your books on the altar when you lit that unity candle. You didn't start a new book together. No, your individual books are still with you everywhere you go, and they govern everything you do.

Your book is called *My Sexual Rulebook*, and it's unique to you. It rules your marriage, including every aspect of your sexual communication. That book is what makes you comfortable or uncomfortable with certain sexual acts and decides how you'll interact with your spouse. It was developed as you were growing up, based on experiences you had in your family of origin, with peers, and while dating, as well as anything that happened to you in the relational realm, especially in the way the opposite gender treated you.

Problem is, most couples have no idea they are carrying that book around or how it affects each of them. It's time to uncover what your book says about your expectations of yourself, the opposite sex, and your relationship.

## Why Mama and Papa Still Control Your Sex Life

Let's take a look at the entries your parents have made in your rulebook. As you grew up, you also developed a life perspective—the way you view yourself, others, and life happenings—as a result of the following.

### How your parents treated you

The kind of relationship you had with your parents has everything to do with how you expect to be treated by your spouse. Which of the following do you most closely identify with?

*The princess/prince syndrome.* Did everything revolve around you as you grew up? Did you get what you wanted when you wanted it? If so, you'll naturally assume that the same techniques will work in your marriage—crying, faking illnesses, throwing tantrums, or giving the silent treatment. However, your spouse was raised in a different home and naturally assumes that things will work differently—the same way they did in his or her home. No wonder there's friction between you.

*The secure, balanced one.* Did both of your parents treat you with respect? Ask your opinion about family outings—but not always follow your wishes? Children who grow up in a home where there is a healthy balance of parental authority, discipline, responsibility, and love tend to emerge as strong individuals who want to give back to the world around them. They also assume that other children grew up the same way, so they have high expectations that their spouse will be just like Mom or Dad.

*The unnoticed one.* Did you grow up in a home where you could have been missing from the dinner table and no one would have noticed? A lot of middle children feel this way. With a "star" firstborn who got a lot of parental attention because he was a super achiever and an entertaining baby of the family who was always up to something, a middle child often feels left in the dust. If you're a middle child, you learned to be more secretive and cautious with family relationships. You didn't say things that would raise a ruckus at home; you settled for the seas of life being smooth. As a result, you may have difficulty expressing your needs and wants in marriage. You find yourself simply going with the flow.

*The inferior/criticized one.* Did you grow up thinking you could never please your mother or father? When you did something wrong, no one needed to clobber you on the head, because you did a good enough job berating yourself. Now you bend over backwards trying to please your spouse. You're afraid to say what you enjoy doing, because no one cared what you thought when you were growing up. You have a low self-worth, so it's no wonder you're uncomfortable telling your spouse what he or she could do to make you happy.

Or, because you had a critical parent, you may have gone the other direction, saying rebelliously, "Who cares? I'll never be good enough for them, so why should I try?" Because of your insecurity, you're critical and controlling in your marriage. *If I'm in the driver's seat,* you reason, *I'll always go the direction I want to go.* Often people who grow up with critical parents end up becoming flaw pickers themselves.

79

If you want to shut off marital intimacy quickly, criticize your spouse. After all, what woman in her right mind would risk wearing something slinky for a husband who eyes her and says, "Well, looks like you've got at least 15 pounds left to lose after having the baby, huh?" Or what husband would risk telling his wife, "I'd really like to try . . ." only to get a dour scowl and a vehement "Don't even think about asking for that!"?

> *If you want to shut off marital intimacy quickly, criticize your spouse.*

*The rock-strewn path.* Some of you experienced a tumultuous relationship with one or both parents, or you may not have been raised with parents. You didn't have the understanding, caring role models you dreamed of. Instead, the adults in your life were distant emotionally or physically, or were verbally or physically abusive. You may have tried to be perfect to please that adult . . . and still failed. Likely, you exited your home with a lot of frustration toward family relationships in general.

If you're a female, you have difficulty trusting men—and that includes the man you married, no matter how wonderful he might be. Often girls who hunger for a daddy's love but don't receive it are catapulted toward any kind of male attention. They spend a lifetime looking for their daddy's affirmation, presence, and acceptance. If he wasn't healthy or available, then he can't be the role model she needs to show her how men should treat a lady. She'll put up with behavior she doesn't deserve because she thinks she's not worthy of being treated right. If this is you, it's not surprising if you've gone through an ex, or a series of exes, to get to the husband you have now—the one with whom you're working to develop healthy marital intimacy. If you're aware of why you hunger for male attention and the trust issues you have, and you share those with your spouse, you can work together to find solutions.

Each spouse needs to know, without a shadow of doubt, that he or she has equal value in the marriage and deserves security, love, and trust.

### What their parenting style was

Were you raised not to cross your dad or mom, who took on the role of the ultimate authority? Were you allowed to ask questions, or were you simply told, "Do it because I said so"? Was your dad's way the only way? Did your mom rule the roost? If so, you grew up in an *authoritarian* home. You were treated as "less than" merely because you were the child. You carry those feelings of frustration and inequality into the marriage, especially if the parent treating you that way was the opposite gender. If Daddy ruled with an iron fist, you as a woman unconsciously project your feelings against him on your unsuspecting spouse.

For example, let's say your husband tells you, "After work tomorrow, I'm going to stop and look at used cars since the Toyota is having issues."

How do you respond? "Fine. Do what you want. You would anyway."

Your husband is stumped by your attitude. After all, you're the one who got stuck on the expressway with the Toyota. He's just looking out for your welfare. But you're responding to his taking control because in childhood, you had no control with your dad calling all the shots.

In contrast, were you raised in a home where, if you wanted something, your mom or dad bent over backwards to get it for you? Did they snowplow your path, making excuses for you when you failed? Did they cover your backside so you wouldn't get in trouble for something you did? If so, you were raised in a *permissive* home. You were used to getting your way. Now, in marriage, if you don't get your way, you're good at pouting or the silent treatment. Your spouse is stumped. *Why is she acting that way? All I said was . . .*

If you were raised in an *authoritative* home, where you were treated with respect, having equal value but playing a different role in the family than your parents, you are much more likely to work together with your spouse in harmony. You discuss issues that come up as they come up, because that's the pattern you saw in your home. Because you had parents who engaged with you in a healthy way, you will tend to:

- be respectful of your spouse and his or her unique role in the home and support it;
- expect more family-togetherness time, because that's what was role-modeled as important in your home;
- work together to get through difficult times and situations;
- be more willing to risk and experiment sexually because you view yourself and your spouse in a positive light; and
- be better able to share your ideas because you see yourself as valuable.

### The way your parents interacted with each other

The patterns you've set in your marriage have a lot to do with the way your parents interacted with each other. Did they treat each other with respect and listen to each other's ideas? Was there a healthy exchange on issues both large and small? Or did one run the home while the other was expected to go with those decisions? How they interacted as male and female helped develop your own perspective about how opposite genders should treat each other. You are living proof of their influence because the rulebook you carried into marriage had everything to do with your parents. If theirs was a negative influence, it's time to pull back the sheets and kick them out of your bed. No one can change the past, but you can make a decision now to think and act differently in your own marriage.

If one of your parents ruled the roost and the other went along for the ride, you grew up with one controller parent and one pleaser parent. If you grew up with two controller parents, you got a hefty dose of people directing your life and telling you what to do. It's no surprise if you feel guilt for never doing enough now and, deep down, you don't feel good enough. If you grew up with two pleaser parents, it's a miracle you learned to tie your own shoelaces and that your family ever got anywhere, because both had difficulty making decisions. They were too busy trying to "please" and make life easy for the other.

Interestingly, opposites do attract. If you're a controller, you likely married a pleaser, and vice versa. Take a careful look at yourself and your spouse. In what ways have the patterns you saw in your parents' relationship carried over to your own marriage?

Men, if you grew up in a home where your dad ran over your mom's feelings and expected her to put up with it, you have a tendency to do the same thing with your wife. It's time to retrain yourself. Each time you start to say or do something, think first, *What will my wife think? How will she feel?* Shower her with unconditional love and acceptance. Ask her opinion. Every day your spouse is longing for approval and acceptance from you—what she didn't get from her parents. She needs your affection and your love.

Ladies, if you grew up always wanting to please your dad, who ruled the roost, it's time to stand up for yourself. Your husband is not your daddy. What you think and how you feel matters greatly. You are half of this relationship. But unless you share what you think and how you feel with your husband, how will he know? He's not a mind reader.

### How your parents treated the topic of sex

Did your parents show positive physical affection—hugs and kisses—in front of you? Or were they stiff and perfunctory? How your parents related became ingrained in you as the way a man and woman should relate. If you grew up in a home where sex was regarded as dirty or distasteful, or not talked about at all, you

## Are You a Pleaser?

- You agree with your spouse so he doesn't get upset.
- You feel like you're never good enough and your feelings aren't important.
- You rarely, if ever, speak up about what you want.
- You can't do enough, even though you're doing more than Superman or Superwoman could accomplish.
- You always wanted to make your father happy so he'd love you. Now you want to make your husband happy for the same reason—to gain his love.
- You always tried to please your critical mother . . . but failed. Now you're trying to please your wife the same way.
- You measure your individual worth by what you can accomplish.

If this sounds like you, you believe your spouse values you for what you *do* rather than for who you *are*. But that's a lie. Don't fall for it. Who you are is valuable and wonderful. You can't always make people happy, and it's not your fault if they aren't happy and don't always like you. You are the one who has to be happy with yourself. Give your spouse the gift of really getting to know *you* by sharing your thoughts, opinions, and desires.

would understandably be uncomfortable with the topic. After all, every time you engage in sex with your spouse, your parents' words or disapproving stares flash into your mind. But portraying sex as disgusting and something you do only to procreate is so far from the truth. It's the most amazing connection a committed couple can share.

If you grew up with Queen Victoria reigning in your home, it's time to cut your mama's apron strings and step away from your father's dour expression when the word *sex* is even mentioned.

Let's say you're in the kitchen, starting on dinner, when you feel an amorous touch. You swivel toward your spouse. "What do you think you're doing?" you spout.

## Are You a Controller?

- You tend to criticize your spouse.
- You almost always get your way.
- You're the one who initiates sex and chooses the sexual position.
- You had a difficult relationship, or no relationship, with your opposite-gender parent.
- You blow your stack easily.
- You have a hard time saying, "I'm sorry. Please forgive me. I was wrong."
- You tend to use the silent treatment until your spouse concedes to your wishes.

If this sounds like you, you live with high expectations of yourself and others, likely because you grew up in a critical, high-stress home. Because you have a need to be right and fear losing control, you hold back intimacy even from your spouse until you're ready to give it. But you're shortchanging the deep relationship you could have by taking a risk with the person you love. Now is the time to take a step back and realize why you are doing what you are doing.

Underneath, you carry a lot of fear. *What will happen if I'm not in control? If I'm not perfect enough? Will I lose the spouse I love?* But when you identify that fear for the lie it is, step back from the control, and allow your spouse her turn in the driver's seat of your relationship, you'll be amazed at your growth in intimacy.

"I just thought since the kids won't be home for half an hour . . ."

You know what your spouse is thinking. *A little appetizer before dinner would be nice.* But there's no way you're doing that in your kitchen. It wouldn't be right. You picture the shock on your mother's face at such a thing.

Wait a minute. What is your mother doing in the middle of your sexual interlude with your spouse? Why is she telling you what's okay to do, what you can't do, and where you can or can't do it? And who says she'd be shocked? Do you really know what your parents did when they had sex?

And you know they did have sex, right? After all, you're living proof they had it at least once.

Who cares what your mother would think anyway? It's your spouse who desires you, so why shouldn't you go for it?

So what do you do next?

You smile seductively. "Just a minute." You turn the burner off on the stove. "I want to give you my *full* attention." And there, right in that kitchen, you take off everything you're wearing and guide your spouse's hand back to where it was.

> *If you grew up with Queen Victoria reigning in your home, it's time to cut your mama's apron strings and step away from your father's dour expression when the word* sex *is even mentioned.*

Oh, the sweet music you can make together in half an hour. All because you decided to shoo Mama out your kitchen door.

And believe me, Mama isn't the only one who needs to be shooed out of your sex life. So many men and women, especially those from conservative backgrounds, settle for less than what they can have because they're so worried about what's "okay" to do in sex and what's not. One woman told me with great disgust after one of my seminars, "There's no way I'm ever going to be on top. That's not right. That's the man's role."

Some people have a narrow perspective on sex that will greatly limit the pleasure they can have. But let me tell you something. Husbands love to be pursued. When a woman initiates sex, showing her desire for her man, that powerful aphrodisiac will keep him coming back for more.

Don't settle for "less than." Go for the wow factor. If you're committed in marriage to each other, and you both agree on what you want to do together, the sky is the limit!

Your sex life is not up for discussion by anyone except the two of you. It's certainly not to be shared with girlfriends over coffee. In fact, ladies, probably the biggest turnoff for men is if you talk about your sex life with your girlfriends. There's a reason a man doesn't like to share with others about his marital intimacy or what goes on in his bedroom. He wants to handle the matter himself.

Honor each other and increase your intimacy by kicking all others out of your bedroom, your kitchen, or anywhere else they tend to congregate. Instead, choose to focus on pleasuring your spouse. Be expressive, be creative. Unleash your charms in every form you can think of, all for the love of the person you married. Learn to let go of your preconceived notions of what sex should be and enjoy exploring together.

If you're a man whose wife came from that "you don't talk about sex and certainly don't do it" background, you need to get behind your wife's eyes. Realize why she's reticent, even fearful, about sex. Then, because you love that woman, be patient and gentle. Make small moves toward broadening your sexual horizons together. Focus happily on what she is comfortable with doing and gain her trust. As she becomes more trusting and less fearful, she'll be more willing to experiment.

---

**Dream On . . .**

- Discover a new purpose for that tent in the backyard.
- Undress your spouse the instant he or she walks in the door.
- Eat a candlelit meal together. Remove one item of clothing after each course.
- Use each other's bodies as plates.
- Spend an entire evening together . . . naked.

If you've wanted to do one or more of these things, or your spouse has and you've turned it down in the past as "not appropriate," why not initiate that act today? Take a risk. Like in the Song of Solomon, let your lover be captivated by you.

---

87

## What Your Life Mantra Has to Do with Your Sex Life

What your parents thought of sex and intimacy, how they responded to your body changes, and whether they discussed or avoided such "touchy topics" have everything to do with what's going on in your marriage right now. That's because their thinking and actions have become part of that sexual rulebook you still carry around. But they've also helped to form something else—your life mantra.

*If you want to know what your life mantra is, just finish this statement: "I only count when . . ."*

Think of your life mantra as the perspectives and life themes you live with every minute of every day. They govern what you think of yourself, what you think of others, and how you respond to others. Those themes also carry right into your bedroom and influence every interaction you have with your spouse.

If you want to know what your life mantra is, just finish this statement: "I only count when . . ."

Take a minute to make some notes. When do you count? Only when you're doing something for the good of others? Only when you please others? Only when people approve of you? Only when you can control the relationship or run the show? Only when you put others first and exhaust yourself doing it? Only when everyone likes you?

Crazy as this may sound, that life mantra you've adopted affects every single thing you do. If pleasing others is the only time you count, you won't be comfortable telling your spouse what you want and need. If controlling others is the only time you count, you won't be comfortable asking your spouse what she wants and needs. See how it works?

So before we go any further, take a short time-out and make some notes. I'll wait right here.

- Identify your life themes.
- How have those life themes influenced your level of marital intimacy?
- What pleasing or controlling tendencies do you see in yourself?
- In what ways have those tendencies impacted your sexual communication?

Discuss your findings with your spouse and do a little brainstorming. How might you take what you've learned and move your marriage to a deeper level?

It's time to kick Mama and Papa out of your bedroom . . . for good. But you can't take the steps to do that until you identify how they showed up there in the first place.

## The Impact of Prior Sexual Experiences

Many of you reading this book have had sexual experiences prior to your current marriage. You may have been married previously. You may have had sex with other dating or casual partners. You may have experienced the trauma of childhood sexual abuse or rape. You may have discovered masturbation to relieve adolescent sexual pressure or oral sex because of peer pressure. You may have been introduced to pornography as a teenager. Some of you have struggled with thoughts of attraction to the same sex and ventured in that direction.

There's a reason our Creator designed sex to be between two people committed in a marriage union for a lifetime. It's because of the intimacy and intensity of the sexual act and the connection it creates emotionally, psychologically, and physically. Think for a moment. What do you remember about the first time you had sex? Was it a pleasant experience? A horrifying one? A disappointing one? Rife with feelings of betrayal and shock? A thrill beyond your wildest dreams? Whatever you encountered during that first time is imprinted on your mind and becomes part of your sexual rulebook. It tells you things like:

- Men aren't to be trusted. They hurt you and betray you.
- Women are objects to satisfy your lust—nothing more.
- Sex is the most amazing thing I could imagine. Worth waiting for!
- Men take what they want, and then they leave.
- Women are fickle. If you don't give them what they want, they'll get even . . . or leave.

Because the sexual act is unforgettable, it makes sense that when you're having sex with your spouse, images of the past will float in front of you—other faces, other times. Just wishing them away won't solve the problem. Berating yourself with guilt for past actions won't either. Accepting blame for being a victim of sexual abuse will only intensify your fear of someone doing that to you again.

*What do you remember about the first time you had sex?*

What will help? Honest communication with your spouse. You don't need to give details. But your spouse does need to know some general information about what happened and why you're responding to him or her the way you are. Otherwise, without the basics, you and your spouse won't be able to come up with what to do so you can get on the same page.

Here are some tips from couples in the trenches:

- "We turn toward each other and focus on each other's faces and pleasure to block out images of old lovers."
- "I tell her how much I love her, and only her. We spend a lot of time in foreplay."

- "She directs what we do. If she's in charge, she feels less fearful and safer."
- "We steer clear of the sexual techniques he used a lot with his girlfriend."
- "When he gets the urge to masturbate, he tells me, and we take care of that need together."

Romantic feelings will ebb and flow. But you can grow your intimacy if you put each other's desires first. That means no holding back—that you're willing to risk, to experiment, in order to fully give yourselves to each other.

*Too many couples who said "I do" now go to bed at night and, by their actions, say to their spouse, "I don't."*

Too many couples who said "I do" now go to bed at night and, by their actions, say to their spouse, "I don't." Don't allow your sexual rulebook— all those dos and don'ts learned from your parents and your prior experiences—to control your relationship. You and your spouse deserve a wow relationship. An experience so sensual that you go to sleep intertwined, thinking, *I can't imagine anything better than this.*

But then the next day it's even better.

## The Five Greatest Elephants on the Couch

Some things never get unearthed in the average marriage, yet they're like the elephant on the couch. The elephant is definitely there, but neither husband nor wife pauses to ask, "Why is that critter sitting in our living room? What caused him to come into our home and sit there anyway?" Both simply walk around the creature, avoid him, and continue to let him sit there, taking up the space they could have to snuggle next to each other.

What are the five greatest killers of a healthy sex life? Unresolved conflict, hygiene, fatigue, a lack of affection and romance, and a lack of caring words.

### Unresolved conflict

Some people tend to harbor grudges and mistrust. If you said something five years ago and it's still a bone of contention with your spouse, that could easily hamper your sex life now. Until you remove that resentment by addressing the issue, your spouse will never be able to touch you in all the right places enough to bring you to ecstasy. Not as long as that issue continues to fester.

Let's say you had a fight with your spouse 24 hours ago. Tonight you had sex. If you're the male, you roll over and go to sleep thinking, *Well, I took care of that little issue.* If you're the female, you're still going over that argument point by point. Having sex didn't solve the problem. In fact, if you weren't in the mood but felt like you had to give it anyway, doing so only made you angrier.

> *Men, let me give you some sage, time-tested advice. If your wife seems angry, looks miffed, or acts annoyed at all, take care of the issue right then.*

Men, let me give you some sage, time-tested advice. If your wife seems angry, looks miffed, or acts annoyed at all, take care of the issue right then. Ask kindly and slowly, "Honey, I notice you seem a little upset. Have I done anything to offend you? If so, I'd like to know so we can talk about it." That snippet of conversation, gentlemen, will win you the Oscar for "Husband of the Year."

In many cases, the unresolved conflict has nothing to do with you. Maybe it was something your father-in-law or a colleague said, or dissatisfaction with life in general. Don't assume the worst.

However, any conflicts or unhappiness will affect your marital intimacy because one of you isn't feeling your best.

Rob and Anna, a couple I know, purchased an older home and were in the process of rehabbing it so their three kids would each have their own bedroom. To do so, Rob decided they had to move the wall in the master bedroom. Six months later, he confided, "I don't know what's wrong with Anna. Maybe she's going through a midlife crisis or early menopause. But she never wants to make love anymore."

When I prompted him to figure out when the change had happened, a light dawned. For six months, one wall of their bedroom had been a thick plastic sheet. Maybe, just maybe, Anna felt a little too exposed to have sex in a bedroom that resembled a greenhouse.

After Rob's eureka, the rehab project progressed like lightning, complete with extra sound-deadening insulation in the new wall. Soon Rob and Anna were back to their usual wow sex.

Sometimes it's the little things that can make a big difference. But if you don't know what they are, how can you fix them? Don't make your spouse guess. Fill him or her in on how you're feeling.

A year after their sex life was renewed, Rob and Anna still call that wall in the bedroom their "sex wall." It's their reminder to always talk about what's bothering them . . . before it can become a major hurdle in their intimacy.

### Hygiene

I just have to say it. Men, if you smell, your body is an automatic turnoff for your wife. Women have an acute sense of smell. Simply slathering on some cologne to cover up your BO won't do the trick.

When you asked her on a date, did you take a shower? I hope so. So why would you not take a shower now before you start the romantic moves? Some 10W-30 motor oil and sweat from your basketball game with the guys after work aren't on the list of the "Top 10 Enticing Aromas for Women."

> *If you stink, take a shower. Give that woman of yours a clean body to lavish her love on.*

Back to your dating days. Did you change clothes, or did you wear the same thing you wore the day before, with only a quick sniff test? So why would you hop in bed with your wife wearing the same pair of Hanes briefs you wore yesterday?

Part of foreplay to women is you cleaning up your act so you look and smell good. To romance your wife, you need to craft a suitable environment, and your body is an important part of that setup.

Why am I addressing men in this section? Because you are the ones whose mothers had to constantly harp on you to take a shower when you were an adolescent. The teenage girls already were taking up more than their share of the bathroom time and didn't need to be reminded. Now that Mama isn't here to do the reminding (you did kick her out of your bedroom, I hope), I'm doing it for her. And since I'm a guy talking to guys, I can say it bluntly: if you stink, take a shower. Give that woman of yours a clean body to lavish her love on.

If you do, you'll be amazed at all the new experiences she'll be open to.

### Fatigue

Fatigue is one of the biggest killers of a sex life. It leads men and women to become couch potatoes who'd rather watch late-night television than enjoy a glorious romp with their spouse. This sex killer hits women the most. It's not that men don't get tired—they do. For sex, though, men only need a place and they're ready to go. Women need a reason, romance throughout the day, and a purposefully designed environment that's conducive to lovemaking.

Even more, the person best equipped to help with a woman's top three stressors that cause exhaustion is her husband! He can spell her with the kids and run errands she can't. And ladies, here's another bonus: if he sees what's on your platter, he won't be so demanding himself. Yes, taking time out of your schedule for sex and making it a priority can sometimes seem like one more thing to do. However, if you have a happy, fulfilled hubby, then you'll have a man who will plunge in and help, and your three stress factors will be greatly lessened. Working together as a couple to solve problems and stresses will make you more aware of, and appreciative of, what each of you does.

And that will lead to more appreciation under the sheets too.

### A lack of affection and romance

A woman in particular needs touches of romance throughout the day to set the mood. But both men and women need affection—kisses, hugs, touches, heart closeness, caring about the little things in each other's day—in order to crave the culmination of sexual oneness. If there's no affection or warmth in a relationship, there's no possibility for sizzle in the bedroom. What man wants to have sex with a woman who puts him off, saying, "Not now, dear," or "We just had sex last month"? What woman wants to have sex with a man who sits in his boxers belching pizza as she runs around taking care of the kids? No wonder she barks a loud "No!" when he approaches her for a quickie before the late news.

Affection is about the little things—meeting each other's needs and desires throughout the day. It's a wife tucking an "I love you" note in her husband's lunch. It's a husband calling to say he'll pick up the groceries so she can go straight home from work.

Romance is the single flower a husband plucks from their backyard and puts in a vase for his wife when he brings her tea in the morning. It's the kiss a wife gives her husband when he arrives home from a business trip, as well as the lingering caress and the promise of more later.

Romance is also thinking in advance of an environment that will please your spouse. Since the majority of couples who have sex don't talk about it, though, many couples have no idea what their spouse prefers in bed.

How much do you really know about what your spouse likes?

- Sex in the morning, evening, or anytime?
- Certain scents and flavors? Body lubricants? If so, which kinds?
- Candles? Dim light? Mood lighting? Darkness? Afternoon light?
- Specific colors of lighting and clothing, or depending on the mood?
- Silk, cotton, or plastic sheets?
- Kissing? Licking? If so, where?
- Getting into bed naked or removing clothing once in bed?
- Experimenting with sexual techniques? If so, which ones?
- Talking or making other noises during sex?
- Specific types of foreplay to get in the mood?

Knowing the answers to these questions and providing romantic setups that include these favorites will go a long way with the spouse you love.

Karen wrote me because she was concerned that her husband didn't seem as attentive and affectionate as he used to be. "I know he loves to see me in a skirt—he says that turns him on," she said.

"When's the last time you wore a skirt?" I asked.

"Well, I'm kind of a jeans-wearing woman," she replied. She hadn't worn a skirt in six months.

"You know what your husband likes, so why not do it?" I encouraged her.

That night when her husband came home, Karen was wearing a skirt. She walked toward him, kissed him tenderly on the cheek, and whispered, "I don't have any underwear on."

Wow, talk about that man dropping his computer case on the floor in a hurry.

See how little it takes to turn your sex life around?

If you've never bought a teddy and worn it, now's the time . . . and make it black, your husband's favorite color.

If you've never worn silk boxers but your wife adores silk, purchase a pair . . . and make it red, her favorite color.

If you've never made love by candlelight, go buy a bunch of candles. They'll be worth every penny when you see the admiration for the beautiful setting in your wife's eyes.

If you've never initiated sex and displayed yourself in all your beautiful nakedness, take a risk tonight. Watch the delight and desire sweep over your man.

If you want a wow sex life by Friday, start by doing a few things differently to up the romance. Give a little, and you'll get a lot.

### A lack of caring words

You go to the dentist every six months to have plaque removed from your teeth. Sometimes marriages need plaque removed too. Plaque builds up in marriages when you volley cheap shots back and forth. If you don't work on removing it, soon you're unable to have any feelings for that person you're married to. Then you announce, "I don't love you anymore." But is that really true? If you got under that plaque, you'd rediscover the original feelings that drove you to fall in love with each other in the first place.

I want you to imagine something for a minute. One week from today, you're standing next to the coffin of your mate. How would you feel? Too many couples spend their time majoring on minors. They pick at each other, getting bogged down in the little things and giving each other grief for them. Here's a wonderful piece of advice for all couples: don't let the sun go down on your anger.[1] If you're upset with each other for any reason, talk it out before you hit the sack. Each day is a new start, and it should be one.

There's no such thing as a perfect person. We're all imperfect beings who get crabby and grumpy. We say things we don't mean. The main thing is that when we're unkind, we say four important phrases and mean them: "I'm sorry. I was wrong. Please forgive me. I love you." And when our spouse has one of those days, we extend grace to him or her.

> *The words you choose to use all day go straight to your spouse's heart and also walk into the bedroom with you at night.*

However, no couple can thrive without caring words. We all need nurturing love and unconditional acceptance within a safe environment. That means criticism and competition have no place in a marriage. As we'll discuss in the next chapter, words are a very powerful tool. They can bring you closer, even driving you to a new sexual peak, or pull you apart in cutting scenes that hamper your willingness to risk with each other in the future.

What kinds of words are you using with your spouse? The words you choose to use all day go straight to your spouse's heart and also walk into the bedroom with you at night. When you open your mouth, do you focus on the short term—what needs to be done or didn't get done? Or do you focus on connecting with your spouse?

Neither of you is like the other. But you need each other. It's what makes the marriage merry-go-round both challenging and oh so fun.

## Making Love with Everything You've Got

This last section of the chapter may make some of you blush. Others of you, especially those from conservative backgrounds, might be downright uncomfortable. But you picked up this book for a reason, right? You want things to be different in your marriage. Otherwise you'd just be channel surfing for entertainment instead of reading this book.

I asked you to set aside your inhibitions for the sake of a growing, intimate relationship with your spouse. So just hear me out on what I'm going to say next. Then you and your spouse can decide for yourselves the direction you wish to take your love life.

Now that you've kicked out the people who've been in bed with you, you've identified what's in your rulebook and the previous experiences that are hampering your ability to enjoy sex, and you're aware of the five greatest sex killers, it's time to start making love with everything you've got.

### Especially for men

Let's be blunt. It doesn't take long for Mr. Happy to get excited. Sometimes you even reach that sexual peak and ejaculate before your wife is ready. It happens to a lot of men. But frankly, your penis is the last thing you should make love with.

Yes, you read right. There are other body parts you should be using first in foreplay with your wife—your tongue, your fingers, your lips, your breath, your teeth, even your feet. So why not get creative and use anything you can think of to pleasure your wife? Most women can't achieve orgasm through penetration; they need stimulation of the clitoris to do so. It takes a lot longer for women to reach a sexual peak and ride those waves than it does for Mr. Happy.

*A satisfying sexual experience doesn't mean you both have to climax at the same time. It means you both walk away sexually satisfied.*

99

A satisfying sexual experience doesn't mean you both have to climax at the same time. It means you both walk away sexually satisfied. So concentrate your efforts on helping your wife achieve her orgasm first. If you do that, she won't care if you come early, late, or at the same time. She'll be too busy loving every sensation.

*Especially for women*

Biologically, a man can quickly cross a threshold where there is no turning back. He will have to ejaculate. This especially happens with young couples, where the man is in his most testosterone-charged years of life. If your husband ejaculates prematurely a lot of the time, there's a great fix for that. If you have a romantic evening planned, as soon as your husband wakes up in the morning, give him a quick preview of what he's going to get later. Expelling some of the semen and sexual tension will assist him in being able to give you the romantic play you're longing for later.

Many women, especially those with limited sexual experience, don't know how best they can reach sexual pleasure. What areas need to be touched? With what kind of touch? In what combinations to get the best result? When in foreplay, encourage your husband to touch you by moving his hand to certain areas and also telling him, "Would you kiss me here?" while pointing to that area.

But sometimes a woman needs to do a little exploration on her own. That means she touches herself in specific areas to see what combinations lead her to climax, so she can be a good teacher to her husband.

Some of you right now are very uncomfortable as you read this. The very word *masturbation* makes you squirm. But please, hear me out.

If a husband or wife uses self-stimulation to avoid intimacy with their spouse, that is selfish and destructive. If they use self-stimulation to figure out how to make the sexual experience more pleasurable with their spouse, then they are doing a great thing—working toward a deeper intimacy and thus strengthening their marriage. They are training themselves to be better lovers. They are, in essence, working out sexually to improve their sexual health.

For those who grew up in Victorian environments, who wouldn't have dared say the words *penis* or *vagina* in their home of origin, self-stimulating exercises may be even more important. If you aren't comfortable touching your own body, you won't be comfortable with your spouse touching you in various areas of your body either. And if you experienced sexual abuse and continually flinch when your spouse touches you in a private area, you will need to relearn some patterns in order to enjoy a rich, rewarding sex life with the person you love. But when you prepare for sex by learning how to best have a climax, you are giving a wonderful gift to your lover.

Why not use everything in your power to create great sex together?

# *Thursday*

## Making Love with Words

Why the words you choose, and how you fulfill them, determine your marital intimacy and shape your sex life.

What's the estrogen-to-testosterone ratio in your family? Ours was always five to two as our kids were growing up. That means I've been navigating female emotions for over four decades with my wife and four daughters. Now I've even added three granddaughters to the mix.

I may be as dumb as mud in some things, but there's one critical point I learned very early on. You don't talk to girls the way you talk to boys.

If you want to tell a boy something, you simply come out with it and tell it like it is. You'll then get a slight shifting of the baseball cap and a nod. That's how you know the boy heard you.

Try that same technique with girls, and they do something shocking—they burst into tears. Even worse, they run to Mama Bear, crying, and in two seconds Mama Bear is hot on your trail, demanding, "Leemey, what did you just say to our daughter?" Then she gives you "the look." That searing "you're in major hot water here" expression. Note that "the look" came even before your daughter managed to get any words out. Still, Mama Bear is certain it was you who caused the flow of tears. That's because the posse mentality reigns in the female world. When girls gather to let a guy have it for hurting a girl's feelings, well, let's just say no male in his right mind wants to be there.

But there are ways that a husband can approach his wife in communication and still keep his manliness intact. And there are things that women need to understand about the way men communicate. It is possible to be on the same page when you understand a few basics.

## Communicating with the Opposite Gender

How different are men and women when it comes to communication styles? Poles apart! In the introduction to this book, I noted how differently the two genders process language and emotions. But here's what you need to know to communicate efficiently and to improve your sexual dialogue.

*Men use grunts; women craft paragraphs.*

Men use fewer words than women. One grunt and the tone in which it's given can be an entire conversation. An exchange of grunts and nods works well between men as a communication style, but women need words, sentences, even paragraphs. Men are uncomfortable with and easily overwhelmed by a woman's flow of words. Is it any wonder, then, that after the first 1,000 words on a subject, our eyes glaze over? We really are trying to listen. But we're still back at the first 100 words you said, pondering the meaning of those, before we can take in the next 900.

> *We're snowed by all you're saying as you jump easily from topic to topic.*

Then you fire the dreaded, emotionally laden barb at our male psyches: "Are you listening to me?"

Of course we are. In fact, we're snowed by all you're saying as you jump easily from topic to topic.

*Men like things streamlined, predictable, and simple; women like variety and multiple choices.*

When Sande and I go to a restaurant we've visited before, I don't even need to look at a menu. If I liked what I had the previous time, I order it again. Contrast that to Sande, who can spend 15 minutes or more ruminating over the menu choices. She also likes to suggest, "Oh, honey, if you got the chicken vesuvio, then I could have a bite."

I look at her. "If you want the chicken vesuvio, then order it."

"Well, I don't like chicken vesuvio," she says. "But if you order it, I could at least have a bite."

Mmm, I've never followed that logic. So I do the husbandly thing to get dinner moving soon toward my stomach. I order the lasagna I want and an order of chicken vesuvio, and my wife orders the dish she wants.

I've also never asked a waiter, "What does that person have on their plate over there? . . . Oh, that looks good. I'll try that."

Me? I can decide on my own meal, thank you.

*Men use "I/me"; women use "we."*

Remember the "I" language men use versus the "we" language women use that I mentioned in the introduction? Even young girls use relational, inclusive language to talk to their dolls and to each other. They skip, laugh, and hold hands anywhere they go. Boys? They walk single file, eyeing or wrestling the competition. Girls talk, negotiate, discuss the possibilities, and make sure everybody is on board with the group's thinking before they act. Doing it solo and beating the other guy out is in a boy's nature.

When a woman understands that a male's "I" language is normal, she's less likely to take personal offense at that "I" focus. Instead, she can view it as his "edge" that helps him provide for her and their family. She can encourage him creatively in that male competitive pursuit while providing balance for what she longs for most: his presence in the home.

> **How to Fight Right**
> • Listen before you open your mouth.
> • Think, *What's going on behind the scenes to prompt this question or action?*
> • Watch your own attitude. It impacts your spouse's.
> • Always remember, your spouse's opinion is as valid as yours.

When a male understands that a woman uses "we" language because she's wired to think and act relationally, he won't be annoyed by her continual use of phrases such as, "I was thinking we should . . ." He'll see her conversation as an attempt to bring the family together to a higher relational level, rather than as a pointed-finger accusation of things he's not doing or not doing well enough.

*Men don't dish about their private lives;
women like to share.*

I once asked a group of several thousand couples, "How many of you women would like to go to marriage counseling this week—if it was free or paid for?"

A sea of hands went up.

But when I asked just the men the same question, not a single hand went up.

That's because there's not a man in the world who would willingly put his hand up in response to that question unless his wife whacked his arm and made him. You see, here's how men think: *Why would I tell somebody I don't know what's going on in my life? I don't want anybody telling me how to do my business. I can deal with my problems myself. No way am I airing my dirty laundry in public.*

Why is that? Don't we men want a better relationship with our wives? Of course! But our competitive nature won't allow us to show weakness.

Case in point, who purchased and brought home this book? Most likely the female. She's the one delving into it first and trying to get her guy interested . . . though the word *sex* on the cover is a helpful draw for the male population.

## Getting Good at Talking about Sex

When was the last time you talked with your spouse about your sex life—what works and what doesn't? If you have to reach back into the dim recesses of your memory—or you can't remember ever talking about it—you're not alone. Most couples spend 99 percent of their times of marital intimacy having sex and only 1 percent talking about it. And by talking about it, I mean discussing your likes and dislikes, where you want to have sex, what you want to do, and whether you're feeling fulfilled or not.

Crazy, if you think about it. You talk about finances, the kids, work, doctor appointments, and what to get for groceries, yet you never talk about sex, even if you're having it a couple of times a week. Why is that?

When couples come to me for counseling due to sexual issues, they say, "Doc, we need some help with . . . um . . ."—furtive looks are exchanged—"our sex life."

*When couples come to me for counseling due to sexual issues, they say, "Doc, we need some help with . . . um . . ."—furtive looks are exchanged—"our sex life." The word* sex *is whispered.*

The word *sex* is whispered. With all the babies born in the world, clearly sex is happening. So why aren't people talking about it?

Sadly, it's because sex to some is either taboo or a joke. But it's neither. It's a critical part of your marital intimacy. If you don't talk about what you like and don't like and what you'd like to try, how can you improve your sexual relationship?

*Be open to suggestions and trying new things.*

There's nothing more enticing—or terrifying, depending on your background and perspective—than a spouse saying to you with an inviting tone, "Do you know what I'd love to try the next time we have sex?"

The problem often comes with the response to that question. Keep in mind that it has usually taken the first partner a while to drum up the courage to even ask the question. If the other partner shuts it down, that will shut down any future talk about sex too.

If your spouse suggests something different to try, at least entertain the idea and respond positively, even if you're not comfortable with it. "Mmm, that sounds like an interesting idea. Tell me more about it, and why it's so fascinating to you."

*Talk straightforwardly about what feels good.*

Tell your husband in advance, "Honey, I can't wait for tonight. I love being naked with you. And I'd love it even more if we can take our time. When you stroke me all over first, like here [do some pointing], oooh, that feels so good and really gets me in the mood to want more of you."

Talk about driving a man wild. That guy will hurry through everything he has to do that night so you two can have all the time you want. Remember that competitive spirit a man has? Well, there are times that edge is definitely in your favor, and this is one of them. He'll take your words as a challenge to make you feel good and will work hard at it.

*Know how to present yourself.*

Want to know how to get your partner in the mood? Then let me ask you: Which of the four sexual languages below most excites you? Excites your spouse?

- Visual (sight)
- Kinesthetic (touch)
- Auditory (sound)
- Relational (emotional care)

If you don't know, you can't create a wow sex life. The best way is to directly ask each other the answers to these questions and have a stimulating discussion. If you're from backgrounds where you didn't talk about sex, though, you may want to scribble your answers about yourself first, then how you think your spouse would respond. Afterward you can switch notes with your spouse and use that as the basis of your discussion. Either way gets the job done. Speaking your partner's sexual language will assist you in presenting yourself to him or her in the most alluring ways.

> *Want to know how to get your partner in the mood? Speaking your partner's sexual language will assist you in presenting yourself to him or her in the most alluring ways.*

Here's what I mean. It's winter in Minnesota where you live, and you're always cold—especially because you and your spouse are trying to save on the heating bill. You tend to wear flannel pajamas and even socks to bed. But one night, because you know your husband's primary sexual language is visual, you decide to surprise him. You crank up the heat so you're warm when he comes home. After he climbs into bed and is ready to turn out the light, you call from the bathroom,

"Wait a minute, honey. Don't turn the light off yet. I have something to show you." You enter, posed in a silky little nothing that spotlights your breasts.

That man of yours will resemble a deer in the headlights, because he's focused on your "headlights." I doubt any of us men could explain adequately what seeing our wife's nipples through fabric does to us. It turns us all googly-eyed and weak-kneed.

If you want to finish reeling your man in, sashay up to the bed, lean over him, and say, "I got this just for you." Let me speak from experience. That man will do anything for you. Use it to school him in some new foreplay you'd like to try.

Gentlemen, let's say your wife's primary sexual language is relational. She's been gone for the weekend with her girlfriends on a twice-a-year getaway. When she walks in the door, what she usually sees is a big mess—pizza boxes scattered half in and half out of the trash, spaghetti smears across the countertop, crumbs scattered and toys askew over the floor, and you nearly passed out on the couch after a 40-hour stint alone with your three kids.

"Honey, what took you so long? I calculated the drive time, and you should have been home two hours ago," you say, exasperated. "And what are you going to cook the kids for dinner?"

What if this is the scene she walks in on instead? The house is spotless. You got all the kids to pitch in to surprise Mom and clean up the house while you cooked one of her favorites, even if it's not quite the way she'd make it. You already fed the kids, and they'll be up only long enough to hug her upon her arrival. The dining room table is set for two with a candle burning, and dinner is in the oven.

"Honey, welcome home!" you say and give her a big hug.

Now she's the one who looks like that deer in the headlights. "What happened here?" she manages. "And do I smell . . . ?"

"We wanted you to know how much we appreciate you," you say and smile. "I'll put the kids to bed. You relax or unpack, and then we can eat. I can't wait to hear about your trip. Okay, kids, say good night to Mom."

That, gentlemen, is a presentation your wife would love. A beautiful environment, delicious aromas from the kitchen, the work she expected to do already done for her, and a husband who is willing to engage her in conversation and wants to hear the details of her trip.

To seal the deal—like she did displaying her headlights for you—tell her after that candlelit dinner, "Don't worry about the dishes. I'll take care of them. I left a surprise for you upstairs in the bathroom."

She looks puzzled but heads up the stairs. You hear her soft "Oh . . ." and know she's found the surprise. You drew a bath for her, added some bath salts, and laid out a couple fluffy towels and a new novel in the series she loves.

Such small actions will make your wife feel special, cared for, and ultimately grateful that she married you.

Sure, she may be so relaxed she'll fall asleep tonight before Mr. Happy even has the opportunity to think about getting happy, but never fear. Women have steel-trap minds for relational details. She won't forget what you did, and she'll be drawn to you like a cat to catnip.

Bet your bedroom will be a lot warmer than that steaming tub the next time you make love.

## Interpreting What Your Wife Says and Does

Because men are simple—note that I didn't say "simpleminded"—and women are more complex, men tend to say what they mean in as few words as possible. Women use a lot of words and descriptions and have connotations to their words that the male gender can miss.

*What she says isn't always what she means.*

The problem comes when we men accept what a woman actually says as the truth instead of reading her body language to realize she might mean exactly the *opposite* of what she's saying. If a woman says, "That's just fine," a man would accept that as the truth and move on. But a smart husband not only listens to his wife's words but looks into her eyes and watches her body language.

Are her words said with a smile, a nod, or a light in her eyes? If so, the action you're suggesting is good to carry out.

Are her words said in a miffed tone, with arms crossed over her chest? Then, uh-oh, buddy boy, do that and you'll be in the doghouse for a while.

I learned the hard way that when my wife asks, "Honey, would you like to get some dessert?" she's really not asking a question. She's saying, in a nice way, "I'm craving something sweet. If you don't get me some soon, I'm going to skewer everybody in this car, including you, because I've had a rough day. Or I might start to cry. And you know how much you like that. So pull over right now and get me that dessert!"

> *A smart husband not only listens to his wife's words but looks into her eyes and watches her body language.*

Women lie all the time—what they say isn't always what they mean. If I just listened to her words, "Honey, would you like to get some dessert?" I would naturally respond straightforwardly, "Oh, no thanks. I'm still full from dinner." And I would drive right past her favorite dessert place.

But because I've been married for over four decades, as well as reared four daughters, I'm now wise about what I should do the instant I hear that question. I know the best plan of action for a happy household is to turn that car right around to her favorite dessert place, usher her inside, and order at least two of her favorites, even if my stomach is still protruding from the dinner we ate less than 20 minutes ago.

*Sharing and beautiful presentation are a fact of life.*
*Accept it and move on.*

We get to the dessert place, and I order a dessert I love. When it arrives, though, I'm not allowed to eat it myself. That would be in bad taste (and yes, the pun is intentional). First I have to offer her a bite . . . or two . . . or three . . . before I take a forkful of it myself. You see, women share their plates of food so they can have a variety and try new tastes. Such a concept is foreign to us men, who are more along the lines of, "Touch my food and you die."

I'm convinced the male instinct to stab someone with a fork if they reach for our plate comes from the cavemen days, where we had to hunt our food. Protecting the catch until we could eat it was a physical necessity for survival. But I can just see the cavewomen. They'd carve up those venison steaks in little medallions, then hunt around the forest for some sprigs of green and perhaps a wild carrot or two to garnish the plate and make it look pretty. Then they'd call over their girlfriends from the caves nearby to check out how beautiful the dish looks. At least I know that's what my wife, Mrs. Uppington, the queen of making things look beautiful, would be doing. I'm okay with an all-yellow meal. My wife wouldn't even entertain such an idea.

Your wife's fussiness about the details could drive you crazy if you let it. But think of it this way. The same fussiness that makes her change the tablecloth and candle color for each season also prompts her to present herself to you in that new negligee. Seeing her like that and knowing she's all yours make the sharing and the fussiness pale in comparison, don't they?

### Light a Fire . . . outside the Bedroom

Send your spouse one card per day that corresponds with the letters of his or her name. For example, if your wife's name is "Sharon," you'd send six cards over six days via mail or email—whichever your spouse prefers. (Now, if your wife's name is Elizabeth Anne, good luck.)

- Day 1: **S**eeing your smile in the morning gives me a reason to go to work every day.
- Day 2: **H**aving you by my side and in my bed makes every day worth celebrating.
- Day 3: **A** woman's love completes a man. I ought to know, because I have yours for a lifetime. What a lucky guy I am.
- Day 4: **R**omance comes easy, because you're so easy to love. What would you like me to do for you after work?
- Day 5: **O**nly you can make my heart smile all day . . . and all night. How about we make some beautiful music together tonight? I'll bring home dinner.
- Day 6: **N**o one in this world is like you, and I'm so glad you're mine. I will love you forever.

## Talking So Your Husband Will Listen

Because there's such a difference between how many words men and women use on a daily basis, here are some basics women need to know to successfully communicate with the quieter species.

### Don't nag.

Nagging doesn't accomplish anything positive. It merely gets your ire up and makes your man more stubborn. It also hurts his feelings. That man desperately wants to please you. Think of a little boy standing in the doorway, holding a flower from the yard out to his mom and beaming because he could give her a gift. That is your husband, only grown up. No, he may not always be the most sensitive person in the world and can come across as a little rough or close-minded. It isn't that we men don't want to try or do better; it's that we're often clueless about how to do that.

One couple I know has come up with a creative way to avoid nagging. The wife asks the husband one time to do something, saying in a straightforward tone, "I'd appreciate it if you could fix the spice rack before Saturday, because I want to bake a bunch of things that day and the spices keep falling out." If Saturday morning comes and the item isn't done, she puts a note on his breakfast plate: "Spice rack?" with a smiley face. The husband realizes, without the wife nagging, *Oops, I forgot to fix it, didn't I?* Then, after breakfast, that's the first thing he tackles. No sharp words need to be exchanged. The reminder is direct, yet not in his face, and done with a kind smiley face.

> *Think of a little boy standing in the doorway, holding a flower from the yard out to his mom and beaming because he could give her a gift. That is your husband, only grown up.*

*Tell us up front what you want.*

Just tell us what you want us to do, and we'll do it. If you want your husband to help solve a problem, tell him that. If you want him simply to listen, tell him that too. "Honey, I don't need you to solve this for me, but I do need your input. I'm feeling emotional about the subject right now, so I would appreciate some clarity from you. You're so good at thinking through situations logically." In the bedroom, if you want your husband to stroke you somewhere specific, take his hand, place it there, and then start the motion you enjoy.

*Be direct in your feedback, and leave the emotion out of it.*

Let's say your husband has forgotten to do something you really needed him to do. Instead of berating him, say, "Honey, dinner is going to be late tonight since I had to pick up the kids after my meeting, so I wasn't able to start it yet." You're not saying, "You doofus, you were supposed to pick up the kids and you forgot. How could you?" You simply stated what you needed to do.

Let your husband draw the conclusion: *Uh-oh, I was supposed to pick up the kids and I forgot.* If you don't give him grief, his deserved guilt will drive him to be extremely helpful in the kitchen and anywhere else. He might even make dinner himself. He'll also be thinking, *My wife is amazing. I dropped the ball and she's not upset. Then again, what does that say about me? Do I drop the ball on her often enough she's getting used to it? Boy, I better pay attention and do what she asks me to the next time.*

Look at all you accomplished inside your husband's head and heart without any accusations or raising your voice.

Remember, we men are streamlined. We love direct feedback and take statements at face value. If you tell us, "Sure, I can do that," we consider it a done deal. We may not hear what follows afterward: ". . . if you can pick up Kenny from kindergarten." If you want us to hear all you say, then rearrange your word order: "If you could pick up Kenny from kindergarten, then I'd be able to pick up the items you need for your work party tomorrow." See the difference? It may be subtle, but it has everything to do with how we men process information and exactly what we hear. So why not bypass all the emotional ruckus?

> *We men are streamlined. We love direct feedback and take statements at face value.*

Smart women realize that the best way to relate to men is to say what they mean, rather than sensitively waffling around the subject as they often do with other women. Even better, throw in a bit of humor to take the edge off. For example: "Honey, I know you've had a busy week, but I really need you to take a look at the toilet that's almost ready to overflow." You grin and add, "Using the bushes out back is a much more difficult option for me." Or you could say, "Honey, I want you to put your arm around me as we're sitting on the couch. Nothing more. I've had a long day, with two people yelling at me about things that aren't my fault, and it was all I could do not to cry. I need your strength tonight."

There's no healthy man on the planet who wouldn't step up to the plate, fix that toilet (or, if you're a non-fix-it guy like me, call the repairman right away), and keep his arm around his wife for as long as she wants if her case is presented like that.

### Don't make us guess.

Be straightforward with the male population. We're not your girlfriends, who will interject statements like, "Oh really? How did she look when she said that? And then what did you say?" We men hate to guess what women want. Frankly, it's emasculating, because when we guess, we're often wrong, and we make the wrong plays as a result.

We aren't your girlfriends—we don't have the legs for skirts. So don't attempt to dress us up in them.

### Give us the highlights.

Men, by nature, want the highlights, the basics of the conversation. We don't want to hear the blow-by-blow of an emotional discussion you had today with someone. "She said 'blah blah,' and then I said 'blah blah,' and then she said . . ." drives a sane man nearly insane. Even if he keeps his wits about him, such discussion will, at the very least, cause him to glaze over until you're prompted to say, "Are you listening to me?" Then he feels bad because he knows you've caught his mind wandering, and you're miffed because he doesn't care enough to listen to you. But—and this is a very important but—we don't want to be left out in the cold regarding the information either, especially if it has to do with family concerns. Just keep in mind that our attention is short-lived. If we want to know more, we'll ask. Otherwise, a snippet of conversation about the matter is enough. However, this practical side of men—listening to the highlights so we're informed and then moving on to the next thing—can often come across to women as "He doesn't care."

"Dr. Leman, he never listens to me. As soon as I start talking, he gets this dazed look," a woman told me. She went on to detail for the next five minutes recent examples of when he didn't listen.

*If you want to talk so we'll listen, use fewer words.*

"When you talk with your husband, do you give him lots of details, like you're giving me? Or just the facts about a situation?" I asked.

She looked confused. "Well, I explain what happened, how I feel about it, and then—"

I cut her off. That's a very male thing to do, by the way. And with this woman's torrent of words, no wonder her husband glazed over. "Try this the next time," I told her. "Give him one basic sentence of the facts, such as, 'My mother is starting to lose track of events in her day, and that concerns me.' Then, when he's ready to know more, he'll ask."

She appeared dubious. "What if he doesn't?"

"Wait awhile. Then put another single statement out there. If you don't flood him with information, he's much more likely to engage and start listening to you."

That's the key, ladies. If you want to talk so we'll listen, use fewer words. It's not that we don't want to listen to you. It's that our brains shut off after a minute or two on a topic, and we can miss key details we should know. Give us the high points, the summary, and exactly what you'd like us to do about the situation, if anything. Tell us kindly and honestly, and we're happy to help you. But throw too much multisensory information at us, and our left hemisphere can't handle the sensory overload.

*Give us even one "attaboy" and watch us perform.*

All it takes is a bit of gentle nudging from you, the woman we love and value most, as well as a few "attaboys" when we do

---

### The Best Ways to Communicate "I Love You"

How your spouse responds to what you say and do has everything to do with their birth order in their family of origin. Here are some quick tips to make your spouse feel loved 24/7.

**For Firstborns or Only Children**
- Encourage risking.
- Welcome your spouse's input.
- Help him lighten up.
- Give details of what you'd like her to do.
- Lavish on your pleasure in words and actions.

**For Middleborns**
- Encourage sharing of feelings and concerns.
- Set aside lots of time for just the two of you.
- Make your spouse feel special, thought of, and included throughout the day.
- Ask his opinion and let him choose—whether it's the restaurant or the type of foreplay.
- Lavish on words and little gifts uniquely suited to her.

**For Lastborns**
- Keep the fun quotient high in your relationship.
- Be open to experimentation.
- Share how important your spouse is to you . . . and how appreciated.
- Make time to learn about his interests and go along for the ride.
- Lavish on the surprises. Babies of the family love them!

---

something well or give it our best try, and we can head in the right direction very quickly. We want to be the kind of guy you want us to be. Your affirmation and approval mean everything to us.

## Why Your Words—and Your Actions—Matter So Much

No matter how long you've been married or how good you think your communication as a couple is, it can always be improved. I had a great reminder of that recently. I was in Alaska speaking when I got a phone call from my daughter Krissy.

"Dad," she said, "Mom is so funny."

"I know she's funny. I've lived with her all these years," I joked. "But what did she do this time?"

Krissy filled me in. Sande had asked if Krissy had taken the garbage down for her. When she said she hadn't, Sande exclaimed, "Well then, someone must have stolen my garbage can!"

I burst out laughing.

Taking the garbage out at our house in Arizona is truly a trek through the desert. Because of the heat—and the coyotes and javelinas that love to tip over garbage cans—we have to keep the garbage in the garage until the night before the collector comes at 5:00 a.m. We roll the garbage bin through two- to three-inch stones that are part of our driveway until we finally hit concrete, then roll it over dirt about the length of two and a half football fields to where we park it for the collector to pick up. Sometimes it's so heavy it takes two people to drag the thing down the long road.

Now back to the phone call. Why had it never entered Sande's mind that her thoughtful husband might have taken care of the garbage for her? It got me thinking: had I dropped the ball lately on those little acts of kindness that made my wife feel cherished?

Building your communication skills as a couple isn't a onetime thing. It's about thoughtful consideration on a daily basis. Sex is an all-day affair. It starts early in the morning with words of kindness and builds up with little actions throughout the day . . . every day.

That's because at the heart of each of us is a longing for connection. To have sexual communication that sizzles in the bedroom, you have to have emotional intimacy first.

So, gentlemen, reserve some of your word count from the day to lavish on your bride, since words are so important to her. Turn your thoughts to home as you leave work. Do little things throughout the day to show your wife you are thinking of her. Cuddle her and talk to her in the language she hears best—emotional connection. Let her be a girl—detail-oriented, relational, and yes, even a bit fussy.

Ladies, reserve some of your energy to lavish on your groom. He needs to know he is number one in your world—that you love him, respect him, need him, and want him. That even if you've been married four decades, like Sande and I have, you still desire him. Use your words sparingly and wisely to connect with your man. Treat his tender, soft heart with loving care. Share his excitement. Let him be all boy—competitive and conquering. Connect with his world wherever possible.

Above all, love each other unconditionally. Words are powerful. They can tear apart relationships, build relationships, and repair relationships. The words you choose to use with your spouse matter far more than you might think. They actually shape your sex life, because the person your spouse wants to please most is you. Every time you speak, you address his or her heart.

When you learn what your spouse needs to hear from you and use your words to create an environment of unconditional love and acceptance, you'll create the kind of intimate conversation that will make your sex life soar.

# *Friday*

## *Spice It Up!*

Why variety really is the zest in the marital recipe . . . especially when it comes to the bedroom.

My wife is the queen of making things taste good. A little pinch of this or that, and out of the pot or oven comes a to-die-for dish. If I tried the same thing, I'd have people taking one bite and grabbing their water glasses.

But there's one thing I do know. Marital intimacy needs some spice too.

As we jump into this chapter, I'm going to make a big assumption—that you'll be willing to try some things. Not every idea will be one you and your spouse are comfortable attempting. Some may stretch the conventions and beliefs you grew up with. But there will be plenty of suggestions you can try to get you on the path to creating the sizzle you long for. Talk together about the ideas and agree on the ones you'd like to try. If you do, I promise you'll have the best night of your lives—definitely one to remember—and dozens more.

## How to Add Zest to Your Sex Life

You now have a lot of valuable information about men, women, your backgrounds, and communication. This chapter will help you pull together all you know to add zest to your sex life in a unique combination that's perfectly suited to you and your spouse. Here are a few tips to start you on your way.

*Realize how backgrounds will affect you
and counteract that.*

I've shared the following story in other settings—when I speak and in another book—but it bears repeating here because the point I want to make is so important.

My wife is as modest as they come. She grew up in a conservative home. When we're in a hotel room and she gets out of the shower, do I see her? No, I see a closed bathroom door in Holiday Inn. She gets dressed in her walk-in closet at home. As a firstborn, she likes things predictable, and she doesn't like surprises. As a baby of the family, I thrive on surprises.

One year for our anniversary, I booked us a weekend at a hotel in Toronto, complete with theater tickets one night and dinner reservations for the next night. I like to eat at 5:00, but I made the reservations for 7:30, since that's Sande's favorite time to eat dinner. I wanted our anniversary to be perfect in her eyes.

That night 7:00 came and went. My bride isn't one who can be hurried, but I was getting antsy, hungry, and worried we'd miss our reservations and have to wait for hours. At 7:30, I yelled at the closed bathroom door in my best manly tone, "Hey, honey, come on out! They're not going to hold the reservation for us all night."

"I'll be right there, sweetheart," she said through the door.

I'm not stupid. After years of marriage, I knew that meant, "Hold your horses, honey. I'll eventually open this door." So I sighed and waited some more, pacing the hotel carpet. Worse, I

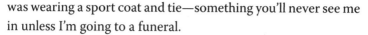

was wearing a sport coat and tie—something you'll never see me in unless I'm going to a funeral.

Finally, my bride opened the door and came out . . . in a see-through negligee. My wife! The Baptist!

I stared and managed to mutter, "I don't under . . . understand."

Suddenly, there was a knock on the hotel room door. Sande hurried back inside the bathroom and slammed the door shut. I still stood stupefied and mute.

At last, after more knocking on the room door, I somehow gravitated there and opened it. A waiter said, "Sir, I've got your dinner. May I bring it in?"

I was shell-shocked. *Dinner? I thought we were going out for dinner.* "Uh, yes, sure, bring it in."

After he exited, Sande came out again in that see-through nightie, holding two little candles. She set them on the table and sashayed my way. "I thought we could eat in tonight."

I said the only thing I could: "Okay."

The rest I won't tell you, except to say our passion built to a new level.

What made it especially exciting to me was that I know that's not who my wife is. But she stepped behind my eyes, knowing that I love surprises. That nightie was, indeed, a surprise. Most of her nighties are flannel and at least five-eighths of an inch thick and rebar-enforced.

And you know why Sande did that for me? Because every day I step behind her eyes. I actively engage with her and show her that she is what matters most to me. I do little things like bringing her a cup of coffee in the morning and putting it by her bedside table because she's a raccoon and has a hard time getting up. I phone her on my way home and say, "Honey, do you need anything from the store?" Understanding each other's backgrounds and perspectives, then meeting each other's needs and making each other feel special, is what marriage is all about.

125

## 4 Ways to Reinvent Your Relationship

- Pretend you're on your first date again. Revisit or re-create the place of that meeting, if possible, and replay the scene, reliving your conversation and those flutterings of interest. Then replay the first time you kissed.
- Wear sexy lingerie under your clothes all day to get you in the mood. Call or text your husband to tell him what you're wearing. Add, "I can't wait until we're both home together." That man will be the first employee out the door at the end of the day, guaranteed.
- Draw a bath and sit in the tub facing each other. Play 20 Questions. Start with simple questions such as, "What is your absolute favorite food?" Progress to "When was the first time you knew you were really attracted to me?" Move into "What's one thing you'd love to do when we have sex?" and then see where that takes you.
- As the two of you are going out the door to a gathering, whisper to your husband, "I'm not wearing any underwear." That man will stick by your side all night, and you can bet it'll be a swift social call.

Because of your conservative background or love handles, you may like the lights dimmed. If so, and that makes you more comfortable, go for it. But why not give your spouse a feast for his eyes every once in a while by letting him see all of you in a negligee that has him drooling?

If your spouse has experienced abuse of any kind, go slow and put him or her in the driver's seat to take any fear away. That builds trust, which will lead to more willingness to experiment and show affection. Choosing marriage for a lifetime means being vulnerable to the one person who has your best always in mind.

*Try different locations and times, and shake up the usual pattern.*

When I first met Jennifer and Martin, both admitted they were bored with their sex life. They'd only been married for a year, but it had become mundane and predictable. Both longed for something more but didn't know where to start. After arriving home around 6:30 p.m., they had dinner together, did the dishes, settled in for a little reading or TV watching, and then headed for the bedroom sometime around 9:30. Then they'd get undressed and have sex before they put their pajamas on.

"Wow," I said, "now that's exciting. You just listed having sex in the same tone as all the rest of the things on your list. Brush your teeth. Check. Have sex. Check. Put your pajamas on and go to sleep. Check. No wonder you're both bored."

To shake things up, I started with their location. They always had sex in their bedroom, after turning down the covers just so and inserting a bath towel precisely in the middle of the bed so they wouldn't have to wash the sheets afterward. It didn't take me long to figure out that both Jennifer and Martin were firstborns—they were precise and perfectionistic and didn't like things messy. That was a big part of their problem.

Here were some of my suggestions to them:

- Walk in the door and engage in foreplay right in your kitchen. Bet those microwave meals will taste even better after that.
- Instead of reading or watching TV on your couch, spend the time exploring each other's bodies and trying out new positions. That book can wait; that TV show will always have a rerun. But great sex only develops when you make it a priority.
- Make love in all the rooms of your house. If you have to drag that towel with you, so be it, but at least change the location (and the towel!).
- At night, throw that comforter off the bed and forget the towel. Chase each other around the whole mattress instead. Then sleep naked, snuggled together in that comforter on the floor. (Sure, you'll have to wash the sheets and the comforter

the next day, but I bet you two could even have fun with that.)

- In the morning, roll over and stroke each other's bodies. Being late to work one day won't kill either of you, and you'll both be smiling all day.

If you're stuck in a boring rut, think about what you usually do. Then change the timing, the location, and your usual pattern. A few minutes of brainstorming can make all the difference in your sexual satisfaction.

*Vary your sexual positions and the type of foreplay.*

Variety is indeed the spice of life, but I want to make one thing clear up front. Love never demands its own way. That means as you experiment, you find new positions and techniques that both of you are comfortable trying. If you've married a "rut man," ladies, remember that you may need to suggest gently that you two broaden your sexual horizons, or he may keep doing the same thing. It's interesting, isn't it, that many women are bored by the lack of variety in sex, and that men get bored and are distracted easily in general? The smart couple pursues sexual experimentation since it solves the boredom factor for both genders.

Most couples settle into a comfortable routine after figuring out what works best with personal preferences and body shapes. But that doesn't mean you shouldn't agree to shake things up every once in a while. You may be open to experimenting but your spouse may not, or vice versa. Just remember that wow sex will never happen unless you both agree to try a certain new position. Here are the four most common positions, with some straight talk about the pros and cons of each:

- *The classic missionary position, with the woman on her back and the man on top.* This is the most common position, for many reasons. It's intimate and tender. The two of you can gaze into each other's eyes, and neither spouse has to be super flexible. However, if the husband is a lot heavier than his wife, she might feel like her breath is getting squeezed out of her. Also, there isn't much stimulation of the clitoris for the woman in this position without foreplay. But if a pillow is placed behind her lower back so her pelvis tilts upward, and the husband rocks back and forth with a downstroke as he penetrates, it's a great hands-free way to orgasm for the wife.

- *Woman on top.* Men love this position, as they get the full view of their bride's gorgeous body. Since a man is tantalized by looking at his wife and seeing her excitement, this ups his satisfaction in lovemaking. There are benefits for the wife too, as she can control the speed, angle, and depth of the thrusting. This may be particularly important if the husband's penis is larger than average, or if his body size is more generous. This position works well for women who are confident and don't mind being on display or are more aggressive. But even for those who aren't, consider this: in this position both husband and wife have their hands free to caress each other.

- *Side by side.* This is a great position, especially for foreplay. If you haven't tried kissing side by side for at least an hour, you're missing out on one of the most passionate acts you can engage in. Most couples tell me that they kissed a lot more when they were dating than they do now that they're married. Too bad! If you want to have incredible marital intimacy, kiss away. Enjoy the sensation of being side by side, skin to skin, and face to face.

You might also want to try spooning, where the husband enters from behind the wife. It's a gentle form of intercourse and works well if one spouse is ill or weary, or if the wife is pregnant. Another option to try is having the husband lift his upper leg and bend it at the knee. The wife then inserts her lower leg between her husband's legs and wraps her upper leg over his body. This positions the penis and vagina right where they need to be.

- *Sitting.* Couples sometimes start in this position because it can heighten flirting and sexual tension. Because you're facing each other, both partners can kiss and have arms free to caress each other. It's a fun way to get things started.

No matter what position you choose—or create your own!—keep in mind the factors of background, any previous experience, and the size and comfortability of each spouse. Also, when one of you is too pooped to whoop, it's only fair that the other one who has more energy be on top and do most of the work.

> *When one of you is too pooped to whoop, it's only fair that the other one who has more energy be on top and do most of the work.*

As you experiment with the different positions, you'll discover that some fit certain moods. For example, if you want to take it slow and sensuously, facing each other side by side might be the best position to start in. If the wife is feeling frisky, having her on top and in control might work well. If you're both in the mood, having the man on top might be just what the doctor ordered.

### Explore and be creative.

Making love isn't only about aligning body parts. It's about intertwining minds and hearts. That's why it's not the position but what you do with the position that leads to thrilling, satisfying sex.

We men honestly don't care where or when or how our brides want to have sex. We're willing anytime. For women, it's all about "the experience." Without the romance, the foreplay, and the right setting, a woman won't be able to drum up the desire. But if she takes on the role of her husband's cheerleader when they make love, that man will do anything in his power to please her.

### Try a little OS.

Have you ever read the Song of Solomon in the Bible? Check out these tasty morsels:

- "His fruit is sweet to my taste."
- "Drink; drink your fill of love."
- "My beloved has gone down to his garden, to the beds of spices, to browse in the gardens and to gather lilies. I am my beloved's and my beloved is mine; he browses among the lilies."
- "Your navel is a rounded goblet that never lacks blended wine."
- "I would give you spiced wine to drink, the nectar of my pomegranates."[1]

I'm not the only one who believes that many of these statements between two enraptured lovers relate to oral sex—stimulating your partner's genitals with your mouth. But even if you don't believe that or are uncomfortable with the concept of oral sex, you still can't miss the love and freedom this couple has to express their passion in thrilling, creative ways.

*Making love isn't only about aligning body parts. It's about intertwining minds and hearts.*

If kissing your spouse on the lips is all right, then why is it not okay to kiss somewhere else? Such as the neck, stomach, breasts, clitoris, or penis? Where do you draw the line on what is okay to kiss and what isn't? A freshly washed penis or clitoris has far fewer germs than the mouth touching it, so it isn't a matter of hygiene.

I've always found it interesting that those under 35 say they have oral sex as often as they have "regular" sex. In fact, when they talk about sex, much of the time they mean oral sex. Those over 35 tend to think of it as "that subject you don't talk about, much less think about." However, oral sex is a great option for older people, for men and women who find it more difficult to climax, and for those who are willing to experiment. I say this with one caveat, though: as with all things in sex, both partners need to find the experimentation agreeable.

> *If kissing your spouse on the lips is all right, then why is it not okay to kiss somewhere else?*

If you'd like to try it out, start at the top of your partner's body, kissing his or her lips. Move down to the breasts or chest, then the stomach. Then scoot down to the legs, slowly working your way up the inner thighs. Be sensitive to your partner's reaction. If he or she seems to want you to go further, gently let your tongue experiment. The most important thing is that you don't push, you don't rush, and if you sense any discomfort, you stop immediately. Some people are not willing to give or receive oral sex. That's all right too. But for those couples who are intrigued by it, these few tips will bring additional pleasure to both of you:

- Stash a cup of hot coffee or tea near your bed and take sips from it.
- Suck on a mint first.
- Let your fingers do the walking and your mouth do the talking.

## Straight Talk about Climaxes

We men love our climaxes. Those few seconds of intensity make it worth all the effort it takes to get there. But what really turns us on is watching our wives turn on. For women, the intensity builds slowly, and many women catch wave after wave of pleasure. Even better, when they finally reach orgasm, women can keep going. So when a man flops onto his back like a limp fish, he sometimes groans to hear his partner say eagerly, "Let's do it again." We men need a little time to regroup.

You see, a woman's body is set up to experience multiple orgasms. In fact, the only limitation on her potential number of orgasms is what she's comfortable with. For many women, one is enough. More than one is exhausting. Other women are happy to ride those waves of pleasure. Women also have more control over their orgasms. They can stop at any point. That's why, when our kids were small, it was tough for my wife and me to have sex at home. One whimper from the baby's crib, and all the foreplay I'd attempted went right out the window. Women have to be mentally ready for sex in order to fully enjoy an orgasm.

Men? They're always ready, and they can control ejaculation until a certain point. However, a man will finally cross a physiological point of no return where, whether he tries to stop it or not, the orgasm will occur. This can especially happen if he hasn't had sex in a while. After two minutes of vigorous thrusting, the average male will ejaculate. It takes the majority of women a lot longer to reach orgasm, and they usually need stimulation of the clitoris.

> *Women have to be mentally ready for sex in order to fully enjoy an orgasm. Men? They're always ready, and they can control ejaculation until a certain point.*

So, gentlemen, if you want another reason for lots of foreplay, that's a good one. Get her ready first, and when you see she's sufficiently stimulated and beginning to climax, *then* begin thrusting.

However—and I want to underscore this—it is not necessary for husband and wife to climax at the same time. In fact, trying to orchestrate that event often puts more pressure on each spouse than necessary and cuts down on their pleasure.

> *Don't make it your goal to force a climax or a simultaneous climax. Simply explore until you learn what types of actions warm you up the fastest.*

Take Ryan and Barb, for example. They'd been married six months when they came to see me.

"I can't get her to climax," he said. "We went to the doctor, and he says she's fine, but something's got to be wrong."

Nothing was wrong with Barb. She was an average woman, slow to climax and needing a lot of foreplay to get there. Ryan was more of a "jump in there and do the job" kind of guy. The more he made it his goal to force a climax on her, the more stressed she became and the less responsive to his touch.

When I explained what Barb needed from him, I could see the relief on her face.

Ryan looked stunned. "You mean women don't always climax? And that's normal?"

"Yes, that's normal," I replied. "But you can turn this quiet woman into a tiger in your bedroom with some gentle stroking and taking your time."

Three weeks later Ryan and Barb came back to see me. This time they were holding hands.

"Wow, Doc, sex is great!" Ryan boomed.

Barb nodded happily.

Becoming a great lover takes understanding, gentleness, time, and a lot of practice. So don't make it your goal to force a climax or a simultaneous climax. Simply explore until you learn what types of actions warm you up the fastest.

### What women need.

Women need a lot of foreplay to get to orgasm. Some women aren't even sure if they have reached orgasm since the intensity varies greatly from woman to woman. It also varies depending on their time of life, menstrual cycle, etc. If you aren't sure if you've had an orgasm, here are a few easy ways to know:

- Do you feel relaxed, calm, and satisfied after sex?
- Did you feel a buildup of tension, an explosion, and then a release?
- Did your body feel like it scrunched up and then finally released?

Foreplay is important for women, but so is the culmination of the sexual act. Foreplay builds up the sexual tension, teasing the clitoris so that a woman's entire body is included in the tension. But culmination of the sexual act brings the release, sexual satisfaction, and drain of emotional tension that a woman longs for.

Will a woman always experience this release every time she has sex? No, she won't. That's why, for women, reaching orgasm isn't the goal. Gentlemen, your goal is to create a warm, intimate, relational experience where she feels cherished and cared for.

### What men need.

For men, reaching orgasm is easy. The problem is prolonging getting there. And it isn't hard to tell when a man has had an orgasm—he ejaculates. There's physical proof.

Remember what I said earlier about women being slow cookers and men being microwaves? Here's another good example, ladies. Your husband has been on a business trip for two weeks. He can barely make it out of the taxi in front of your home without Mr. Happy standing at attention, all because he simply *thought* about having sex with you. With two weeks of him being out of your bed, his sexual energy is heightened. But you? You're like a bear in the winter, gone into sexual hibernation while he's away.

> *For men, reaching orgasm is easy. The problem is prolonging getting there.*

The two of you go into the bedroom, and he's already erect, even without a touch from you. But you take a long time to warm up. Just as you're starting to get there, he orgasms. How you both handle such a situation has a lot to do with how warm and intimate other aspects of your relationship are.

The smart wife might say, "Wow, you really were ready to go, huh? Well, wait just a minute, and I'll show you a few more surprises. I might need a bit of your help, though." That's when you stroke him, kiss him, and then guide his hand and other body parts right where you want them.

The husband who knows he is safe in his wife's love might say, "See what you do to me? I couldn't help thinking of you all the way home, and this is the result. I'd like to make you happy. What would you like?"

That's a couple who turns a situation that could be tense and embarrassing—if you aren't comfortable with each other—into a fun event that draws them closer.

For men who continually ejaculate prematurely, there's a simple exercise that will help. Clench the muscles that you would if you wanted to stop urinating midstream. Those are your PC muscles. Two or three times a day, contract the PC muscles 10 to 20 times.

Every few contractions, hold for three seconds. You can do these exercises anywhere—even at your desk at work—with no one noticing. But within a couple of weeks, I guarantee your bride will notice your skill in the bedroom.

Just think of the fun you can have as active participants, giving to each other with uninhibited passion and using your best male and female skills to pleasure each other.

For women, use your unparalleled communication skills to tell your man exactly what feels good to you. It's better than him hoping he hits the right spot and missing it by a quarter inch. Simply take his hand and move it where you want it to be. Then encourage him with your words. "Right there, honey. Yes, that's perfect." He'll love watching you take pleasure in his attentions, and that will heighten his own pleasure in lovemaking.

For men, start easy, slow, and soft. Give her the time she needs to warm up first. When your wife crescendos toward a climax, pour on all the passion she wants.

It takes two to do a marvelous tango. But after today, you'll have all the info you need to develop your own passionate dance. So what are you waiting for?

*Bonus Features*

# Romance on a Budget

If you want an evening at home all to yourself as a couple, and you are on a limited budget and have children, you can try a wonderful invention. It's called a parent co-op. No money is exchanged. You swap evenings of child care or receive credit hours for taking each other's kids. Here's an example of how it works for four couples I know, who have limited incomes and a total of seven kids between them. Each couple has all seven kids at their home on one Friday night a month. That means all the couples have three free Friday date nights every month.

*The Washingtons* try out different restaurants, especially unique, ethnic ones. They set a $20 limit for themselves and enjoy whatever fits within those parameters. Thus far, they've enjoyed Indian, Mexican, Chinese, Polish, Italian, and Vietnamese. Next on their list is Thai food. But their favorite part of the evening is the romantic, hand-holding walk afterward to work off the food. Seeing the stars overhead and getting fresh air catapults their sexual energy into overdrive. "We're usually running toward the car," Jim reports with a grin.

*The Pendletons* take a different night class together from a local college every semester. Over the past two years, they've done mamba dancing, ceramics, Chinese cooking, and social networking (so they could be on the same page as their technologically savvy kids). This semester they're taking a gourmet desserts class. Three of the four nights are covered with their babysitting co-op. The other Friday night the kids are with Grandma and Grandpa, who take them once a month for the weekend.

"The mamba dancing especially paid off," Rhonda says.

"Yeah," Jason adds, "now we've got some new moves for the bedroom." He winks at his wife.

*The Ashtons* specialize in "under five bucks" date nights. They set aside a $5 bill and think of fun ways to spend it. Often they don't even spend it at all. Here are some of their ideas:

- Rent a dollar movie (we especially love the old 1980s movies since the clothing and hairstyles add humor to our evening) and make different kinds of popcorn. Thus far we've tried cheese, caramel, turtle, peanut, and fruit popcorn. We love to sit together, feet intertwined. Before long, we have that movie on pause and are trying all kinds of fun things with that popcorn.

- Buy a scented bath pack and enjoy a long soak and talk together. No cell phones allowed. We make sure there are lots of towels nearby, in case we decide to slide out of that tub and make a love nest right on the floor.

- Look for cheap deals or coupons at drive-throughs, like 49-cent cones and 99-cent hot dogs. Drive to a park, sit in the backseat, and enjoy those special deals with a lot of kissing. It'll make you feel like teenagers again.

- Buy one meal deal that's under five bucks and feed bites of it to each other. Hold hands and gaze into each other's eyes. It won't be long before you're out the door of that fast-food restaurant to sample some dessert (and you know what we mean).

- Buy vanilla ice cream and two cans of root beer to make root beer floats, some chocolate syrup or strawberries and whipped cream to make sundaes, or fruit to make smoothies if you want a low-calorie version. Draw the kitchen shades and make your dessert . . . naked. Bet you can find lots of fun things to do with the ingredients along the way. We always do.

*The Andersons* are on a very tight budget with Mark's company in transition, Kim just beginning a part-time job, and six-year-old twins who have special needs. But Kim and Mark are also very inventive. On the night they have all four couples' children, they make pizza dough from scratch, and each of the kids gets to make their own mini pizza. The ingredients are inexpensive since the Andersons shop at a discount store, the kids have a blast making their food, and every child enjoys eating their own handiwork. All seven kids look forward to that pizza evening once a month, and the twins love having other kids to play with.

On Kim and Mark's date nights, they pull out their brainstorm list. Here are a few of the free things they've enjoyed that have drawn them closer as a couple:

- Slow-dancing in the living room to a wide selection of retro records, with candles scattered around the room.
- Walking in the rain and stripping each other's wet clothes off afterward.
- Giving each other a foot rub. Then slowly making our way up each other's bodies.
- Making snow angels, building snowmen, and having a snow-ball fight. "There's nothing more romantic than chasing each other around the yard, stuffing snow down each other's shirts, and then running inside to retrieve that snow from where it now resides," Mark says, grinning.

- Drinking hot chocolate and letting our warm hands and tongues wander while watching borrowed movies from our movie co-op.
- Playing strip hide-and-seek. Each time a hiding place is found, that person has to take off an item of clothing . . . or, even better, the spouse gets to choose what to take off his or her partner.

Why not come up with your own romance-on-a-budget list?

# Surprises Your Spouse Will Love

You plan a lot of things every day, so why not plan one sexual surprise a week? Your spouse is worth it, and it will take your lovemaking to new heights. Here are a few ideas you might want to try:

- If you're a woman, remember this secret: we men would rather our wives come to bed with clothes on. Why? Because we like to take them off! When you wear some surprising lingerie, that tells us you've thought in advance about surprising us, shopped carefully for the item, and planned a wonderful time to model that new purchase for us. Setting aside a little money once in a while to buy lingerie will keep that man guessing, stimulated, and eagerly in your court.

- Eat foods that will help get you both in the mood: strawberries, chocolate, seafood (especially oysters). Even better if you use your naked stomachs as plates.

- Place a candle or two or three in the room. How many you use and what color they are can create a completely different ambiance. White suggests slow, leisurely love. Red suggests, "Come and get me—fast." Yellow might be for a playful mood.

- Buy some special sheets for your wife, since the touch of her naked skin on them is especially sensuous to her. Don't just give them to her; put them on the bed yourself so she's surprised when she slides in. Choose cotton for long, lingering sex that could go all day or all night. Silk might get things going right away. And if you want frisky, try a plastic sheet and a bottle of baby oil.

- Men are turned on by sight, so let your husband undress you right in front of a mirror to take in all the beautiful aspects of you. Even better, put a soft blanket right by a mirror and make love in front of it. Your enjoyment will be higher because you'll see how enraptured he is by you. And that man of yours? His excitement will be to the moon because he gets a 360-degree view of his woman.

- Stir up a hot chocolate bath, using three tablespoons of cocoa, one tablespoon of powdered milk, and, of course, hot water. Add a little whipped cream if you'd like. I guarantee you won't mind rinsing out that tub later.

- Consider a twist on giving your wife flowers. Place a single rose by the bed, but then use the others to create a scattering of rose petals under the sheets. The aroma will please her nose, and I'm sure you can think of lots of ways to caress her body with those soft, silky petals.

- Try a new scent. Tell your husband, "I hid a surprise scent for you somewhere on my body. It's your job to find it."

- Never throw out an old pair of underwear. Put those underwear on, sashay up to your spouse with a pair of scissors, and dangle them in front of him or her. Say, "If you can get these off me, I'm all yours."

- Explore your kitchen for tantalizing possibilities. Whipped cream, chocolate sauce, maraschino cherries, maple syrup, and frosting make wonderful hors d'oeuvres in foreplay when added to just the right body parts. Licking them off with your tongue is a lot more fun than eating a sundae with a spoon.

# Ask Dr. Leman

Straightforward answers to the hottest questions couples ask about sex and intimacy.

Admit it. You have some great questions you're dying to ask about sex, intimacy, and life as a couple—things you've always wanted to know—but you don't know who you can ask. In fact, you're a little embarrassed to ask. With me, you can put aside any embarrassment and just be blunt. The questions you have are likely ones that thousands of other couples ask as I interact with them on a daily basis in my speaking, counseling, and writing. For over four decades I've been thrilled to watch couples use the principles in my books to develop an intimate connection, to broaden their communication, and to fine-tune their lovemaking to an art form that rivals Picasso's and Michelangelo's. I want to see you and your spouse do the same thing. So, in this section, allow me to be your personal psychologist and "love doctor."

For additional help on specific topics, consult "Resources by Dr. Kevin Leman" on page 282 and follow me on Facebook and Twitter. If you don't find the answers to your questions, zip me a note on Facebook, and I'll be happy to answer for your own and others' benefit. For every person who has the guts to ask a question, there are myriad others who want to know the answer too.

If you want great sex and fabulous communication, you can have all that.

So go ahead. Plunge in. An intimate connection, more satisfying than you could ever dream, awaits.

# Introduction

## Vive la Différence!

Why men need women, why women need men, and why a good sex life is worth striving for.

### Prewedding Jitters

**Q:** We're going to be married in two months. Part of me can't wait, and the other part is scared stiff. The closer that wedding date comes, the more I realize how different we are. Guess maybe I'm getting the prewedding jitters, even though I love my fiancé with all my heart. Is it normal to get worried about stuff like that?

**A:** Of course you're different. Men and women are different. If you were both the same, one of you wouldn't be needed. It's those differences that make your life together full of exciting surprises. What fun would it be if you were married to someone exactly like yourself? Becoming a couple means two people with differing backgrounds, gifts, and personalities coming together.

Not only that, but men and women have very different needs.

Women want three things: affection (closeness and cuddling, not necessarily sex), communication, and a commitment to family. That means it's important for your husband to snuggle you, talk with you, and also be where he says he'll be, whether it's a dinner party for your work or picking up tacos when you're running ragged.

Men want three things: to be wanted (to know you desire them physically), to be needed (to know they matter, that you need them in your life and their role is unique), and to be respected (to know they are the rock of the family, your problem solver).

With such varying needs, is becoming one easy? No, but here's a secret that works every time. Get behind your spouse's eyes and see how he views life.

There's something you should know, though. It's easier for a woman to get behind a man's eyes than for a man to get behind a woman's eyes. That's because a female's view of life will probably change more than a male's along the way. We men tend to be creatures of habit. We live life more simply. Since we're not as complex as women, our perspectives often stay the same. A woman's can differ greatly depending on the current situation she's in and how she feels about it. I pointed out these differences in my book *Under the Sheets*, where I said to think of your husband as a four-year-old who shaves.

But if you recognize and celebrate your differences, and get good at seeing life from behind each other's eyes, you'll have a wonderful marriage, where you can have fun growing together.

Enjoy the ride!

## All Guys Think about Is Sex

**Q:** A girlfriend once told me, "All guys think about is sex." Is that really true, and if so, how can I turn his attention to other things? Thinking about sex all the time can't be a good thing . . . or is it?

**A:** Yes, guys think about sex. But it's not the only thing we think about. We think about food, ESPN, and sports too.

Seriously, men do think about sex a lot more than women do. But how much more? Take the following pop quiz to find out. Go ahead. I'll wait for you, and no peeking at the answer until you're done.

Men think about sex . . .

- Two times as much as women.
- Five times as much as women.
- Twenty times as much as women.
- Thirty-three times as much as women.

And the answer is? Thirty-three times as much.

*That's sick*, you might be thinking. Well, my wife said the same thing when I told her. However, it's not sick if when he's thinking about sex all day, he's thinking about you . . . dreaming about kissing your neck, disrobing you, giving you pleasure. That is good and healthy for your husband to focus on and cements your marriage bond even more because you are an active image in his brain. As your husband thinks about sex 33 times a day, he thinks about you 33 times a day. Now that's a different perspective on his sex-laden thoughts, isn't it?

## I Can't Stop Looking at Other Women

**Q:** I am happily married and sexually fulfilled by my wife and always have been in our two-year marriage. But every time we go out for dinner, I can't help but notice women who are nicely endowed as they walk by. My wife catches my eyes straying and gets really angry that I'm looking at other women. Last night she said, "What? Don't I have big enough breasts for you?" I try to stop, but somehow I can't. What's wrong with me? My wife is the only woman for me, but she's getting more and more frustrated. Other than wearing a bag over my head so I don't see anything, what's the solution?

**A:** Guys are like squirrels, attracted to and distracted by anything shiny. We're innately wired to notice the opposite gender. After all, that's how your wife caught your attention, right? You can't help but see the female species. What's most important is what happens next. If you are happily married, you will think, *That woman has some amazing features.* You will admire them for a moment, yes, but then you'll think, *Still, I've got the best woman of all. Mmm, in fact, that outfit she's wearing right now is pretty sexy. I wonder how long it'll take me to get that off her once we get home. . . .* And you turn your attention back to your wife.

Your wife needs a Guy 101 course on the fact that men are visually stimulated. We do look if a pretty young woman enters our office or sashays down the street. However, being visually stimulated and wanting a relationship with that person are completely different things to men. Because women are relationally stimulated, the first thing that will jump to her mind is, *Oh, so you think she's sexy. You want her more than me.* That's not what's on your mind at all. The woman who walked by might have some great headlights, but your wife's headlights are all yours to explore.

May I suggest something else too? To ease the tension, whenever possible choose a booth where your eyes can focus solely on your wife. In other words, sit where you face a back wall and can't see who is coming in and out of the door. That will help your eyes not to stray so you can enjoy your meal with no simmering indigestion for either of you.

## Sex in the Morning—or at Night?

**Q:** My husband likes sex in the morning. He says he has more energy then and feels more fresh. I beg to differ. I appreciate a freshly showered husband. Any hint of BO makes me want to run. (I hate the slight smell of garbage in the kitchen too, which is why we have a miniscule garbage can and the contents go out of the house twice a day.) That's why I like sex at night. He always comes home and showers after work. Just the scent of his Herrera for Men turns me on if I catch a whiff of it. Plus, to me, nighttime is more romantic with dimmed lights. We never seem to agree on when to have sex. So who should win?

**A:** Why does someone have to win and someone have to lose? Why not make it a win-win for both of you? Take advantage anytime the urge strikes. Tell your husband up front that you need him to take a shower. That any armpit smell makes you not as eager to engage. If you compare it to how you feel about the kitchen garbage and explain kindly how sensitive you are to smells, he'll clearly get the picture without being offended. (You're not the only woman who is sensitive to smell. I have a daughter who has a nose like a German shorthaired pointer on the scent of a pheasant. She can identify any aroma—good or bad—from 50 paces off.)

Also tell that husband of yours that the scent of his cologne turns you on. I assure you he'll be ordering more from Amazon to stock up. And I guarantee that he'll pop out of bed like the Energizer Bunny and sprint for the shower when he wakes up, so he'll be fresh for you. Why not have sex in the morning and sex at night too? Problem solved. Just realize that if you want the whole enchilada, it sometimes takes men, especially older men, a bit of time to regroup.

## Is Sex Necessary for a Happy Marriage?

**Q:** Sex hasn't been high on either my spouse's or my agenda since we got married. We've always been good friends and have had a wonderful marriage for nine years. Even the first year we were married, we only had sex a few times, when we planned a romantic weekend. We're both okay without it. But sometimes I wonder. Why do people say sex is such an important part of marriage? Is it really, or is that Hollywood hype? Do you need sex to have a happy marriage?

**A:** It sounds like both of you have low sex drives, or one of you is lying. Have you and your husband discussed your sex life? Is he happy with the way things are? A man's basic needs are to be wanted, needed, and respected. And yes, sex is part of being wanted. If your man is sexually fulfilled, he will be your hero, knocking down walls for you. He'll do anything you ask. He'll hold you when you vomit. He'll do errands for you. He'll walk on water for you.

If you have that kind of a man already, then you have a one-in-a-million partner. If you don't, the way to get him on the same page as you is to provide him with a sexual experience he won't forget—complete with anticipation, foreplay, and the culmination. Sex is the physical glue of marriage. It makes you stick together when times are good and also when times are difficult. It's an important part of becoming one. But sex also requires vulnerability, and that may be something each of you isn't comfortable with. You said you were "good friends." That makes it sound like you are roommates playing house. But is that what each of you truly wants? Wouldn't you rather have an intimate connection that draws your hearts together, even when you're not physically in the same room? That's the result of a healthy sex life. To get there, however, you need to discuss both your expectations and your desires.

### Romance = Sex . . . or No?

**Q:** Does romance always equal sex to guys? The only time my husband gets "romantic"—kisses my neck, brings me flowers, or runs an errand for me—is when he wants some nookie at the end of the evening. Why can't he do things for me just because he loves me, sees I work hard, and wants to be nice and give me a break? We've been married for seven years, so you'd think he'd get it by now, but no. How can I get him to see that, for me, romance is a lot of little things?

**A:** Every day a woman asks her husband, "Do you really love me? Do you really care?" How she feels about the answers to those questions has everything to do with the things a man does during the day. If your husband only does things so that you'll have sex with him, you're not feeling loved because he's not meeting your other needs. Have you ever told him that sometimes you just need his help? That you would feel better about jumping in the sack with him if he extended more loving gestures to you along the way and helped out around the house?

Husbands want to be needed—to know that their role in the family is important. Could you perhaps be too competent, not allowing him to help or unwittingly leading him to believe you don't need his involvement? Women can zip circles around men when it comes to multitasking. In fact, you can be downright intimidating to a man who works hard at doing one thing. If you've never talked about this, it's time to do so now. What would you like your husband to help you with? What do you like to handle yourself?

Also, explain to him how much the small things—a kiss on the cheek, his arms encircling you from behind when you're stirring something on the stove, him calling to see if you need something from the store—mean to you. Be honest and say it's hard to drum up the mood to have sex if you haven't experienced romantic gestures throughout the day.

Guys in general are completely clueless about what a woman wants unless she states it straightforwardly. We don't like guessing, and we're not very good at it. But if you tell us what to do and how to do it (nicely, of course), we're more than happy to oblige. We really do want to please our brides. That's important to us.

## Opposites Attract . . . But Now What?

**Q:** We come from totally opposite backgrounds, and we haven't found marriage easy. In fact, the differences that attracted us to each other and made dating exciting are making our relationship hard now. We see life very differently. Yet we've both agreed that we're committed to this relationship no matter what it takes. We're not the kind of people who give up on anything, much less each other. But how can people who are so completely different find common ground? Where can we start?

**A:** Good for you for staying committed to each other and for wanting to work things out. After all, you chose each other. Your tenacity says a lot about both of you and your character. That means you've got great material to work with. My guess is that you had a fast courtship, with a lot of romance and not much time to discuss how your backgrounds affect you. Now's the time to change that. Arrange for date nights where you discuss one topic in depth, such as:

- How would you characterize your relationship with your dad?
- How would you characterize your relationship with your mom?
- How did your parents treat each other?
- What core values did you grow up with?

- If you could change one thing about your growing-up years, what would that be, and why?
- How is each sibling like you and unlike you? Which sibling is most comfortable for you to be around? Why?
- What are two of your favorite memories from growing up?
- What's your earliest childhood memory, and why do you think you remember that?
- What's one time you felt judged and misunderstood? Why did that bother you so much?
- At what point(s) in life did your life mantra or perspective change, or your thoughts of what might happen in the future?
- If you could engineer a perfect day, what would it look like?

Because your backgrounds are poles apart, you better get good at figuring out where both of you came from since it's likely you'll view the same event from very different perspectives. All of the above topics, as well as many more you can brainstorm, will assist you in viewing life from your spouse's perspective.

Can your marriage work, and work well? You bet!

I believe God was the original humorist when he came up with "The two shall become one." Seriously, that's funny. Yet it wasn't a suggestion. It was a command. Is it easy? No, especially for people like you, who have widely varying backgrounds and have to work on finding common ground. But it's worth the effort. My wife, Sande, and I are living proof. When I met her, she was a classy, beautiful nurses' aide who had a firm faith in God Almighty. I was a janitor who had been thrown out of college. I had no direction for what I wanted to do, no real prospects of going anywhere in life. And although I'd grown up in the church (my mom dragged me there), God had no relevance or place in my heart. Somehow, in God's irony, Sande and I fell in love (to this day I consider that a miracle), and as we became one, I was motivated to become the person I am today. In fact, decades later, she still motivates me to become a better human being.

So stay committed, keep talking, and view the world through each other's lenses, and you'll change the world together.

# Monday

## Why Women Need Sex

Why sex is integral to a woman's life, what she wants most of all, and what stops her from wanting sex.

### Too Pooped to Whoop

**Q:** I'm a stay-at-home mom, and we have three young kids. My husband comes home from work, eats dinner, and then watches TV for a couple of hours to wind down. In the meantime I'm stuck with the cleanup, the kids' baths, putting the kids to bed, etc. When I finally get them tucked in, I'm exhausted. A fling is the last thing I want. A foot rub and a shower is more like it. Then again, being a mom is my job, and his is working all day. Still, I can't help but feel a little touchy about it. Am I way off here in expecting some help?

**A:** You're not way off; you've hit the nail on the head. And of course you're touchy. You made the difficult decision to stay home and take care of those kids, and that job is 24/7. You can't do that without some relief. It doesn't help that your husband expects you to fulfill not only all the kids' needs but his too. So he works a 9-hour day; you work a 24-hour day. Chances are, you're the one who also gets up with the kids at night.

It's time to take a stand—and to stand up for yourself. When my wife went to a ladies' group for three hours when our two girls were very young, I thought she'd been gone for three days instead of three hours. I was utterly exhausted by the time she got home. Those several hours gave me an incredible appreciation for all she did and kicked off my idea of taking our kids out for a few hours every Saturday morning so she could sleep in.

Your husband needs a good dose of reality. Running in your sneakers for a while will give him a firm grasp of what you do. Then things will turn around in your house.

So do this. The next time he's in the house with the kids, quietly stash everything you need for the next three hours in the car. Then tell him, "Okay, I'll be back in three hours. You're on to take care of the kids." Then make a swift and gracious exit before he can argue.

I can guarantee that for the next three hours he won't be snoozing in front of the boob tube. He'll be running point with all three of your kids and too pooped to whoop by the time you get home. You, on the other hand, will feel fresh as a daisy after time by yourself. When he gets the picture of what you do all day, he'll be much more helpful with the kids and around the house, and you'll have more energy for that bedroom activity he has in mind.


## His Ex Is Gorgeous

**Q:** I was cleaning out some memory boxes a month ago when I came across a picture of my husband with his ex. His really gorgeous ex. Complete with perfect body in a red bikini on a beach. I felt sick inside. I'm just average, and I definitely don't look good in a bikini. I can never be her. Since I found that photo, sex hasn't been as fun because I'm always thinking, *How can I ever measure up?* She's always floating around in the back of my mind. I feel so . . . plain next to her. How can I get over that feeling so I can enjoy sex again?

**A:** It's human nature to compare ourselves to others and think the grass is greener on their side of the fence. Sure, your husband's ex might be gorgeous. But he's not with her now, is he? He's with you. He chose you. That means you have something his ex didn't, and that's what attracted him to you. You don't have to measure up to her; you never did. You may not have a perfect body in a red bikini, but you can set up a tent in the backyard and create a blissful experience all your own. Let me tell you, the word *plain* won't even enter your husband's thoughts inside that tent . . . or anywhere else you're together either.


**He Forgot Our Anniversary!**

**Q:** I'm crushed. We've been married three years, and my husband forgot it was our anniversary. How can he remember the scores of the last NFL game and forget the day we got married?

On our first anniversary, he booked a romantic restaurant, got down on his knees, and gave me a diamond heart necklace because he said I'd captured his heart. For our second anniversary, he hand-delivered a dozen red roses with a note that said, "I'd marry you all over again," brought home my favorite takeout food, and set up a romantic dinner with candles on our deck. This year . . . nothing. He didn't mention it at all. Even me wearing a hot new nightie didn't flag the event for him. I didn't say anything; I don't want to embarrass him or make him feel bad. But what happened? Is our marriage not important to him anymore?

**A:** Hey, he's two for three. You know, if he keeps that up, he'll be in the Hall of Fame!

Some guys miss things like holidays. Believe it or not, some even miss Valentine's Day and Mother's Day. I know you're hurt. But it really isn't anything personal. Your guy isn't a multitasker like you are. He thinks of one thing at a time. If something is heavy on his mind, he may not even remember what day it is, as much as he loves you. Give that guy of yours a break. Thinking of those romantic gestures for your first two anniversaries is definitely not the normal "guy thing" to do. Briefly mention that he forgot your anniversary, which was a disappointment to you, but then move on. You've got a keeper.

This is what I'd do. Start a calendar on Google Drive and add any event that you want him to remember. It will then pop up on his phone or computer. Make the reminders playful and give him a couple days' notice, so he can plan (we guys like to plan). "Anniversary #3 in two days . . . counting down to some major fun!" The next day: "Anniversary #3 tomorrow. Can't wait to model the hot new nightie I bought for you." And then, on the actual day: "Happy #3 anniversary, hon! I'd choose you all over again. And I can't wait to show you how much. PS: The new nightie is a fiery red, and there's not a whole lot of it. See you soon."

Here are some alternate fun ideas for the night before your anniversary or the morning of:

- Write a message and attach it with a safety pin to the zipper loop in his pants (he can't miss that!): *For the love of my life. Happy anniversary.*
- Leave a card where he gets dressed in the morning and inject a little humor: *Just think—it was three years ago that*

*we pledged our troth to each other. By the way, honey, do you know what "troth" is?*

- Prop a card by the coffeemaker that says, *Happy anniversary, darling. Hurry home, because I'll be waiting for you in a very special outfit.* Your husband will do his work in double time to hustle home.

If that guy of yours has completely forgotten what day it is when he sees your message, he has at least 9 or 10 hours to come up with something. Remember, he's doing it for you.

Now isn't that a lot more fun than being miffed that he forgot your anniversary? I bet that man of yours will come up with a few surprises all his own. Men are predictable; they will forget. However, if he sees an event on his calendar or you flag it with a note, then that logical man has the opportunity to plan ahead. That's a bonus for both of you.

A man gets high A's in scoring from a woman if he thinks through an event, initiates it, plans it, and gives it his best effort. So why not give your guy the chance to do that rather than feel like a schmuck when he realizes he forgot?

A calendar of events (thanks to my smartphone) keeps me in sync with all the happenings of my wife, each of my five kids, my three sons-in-law, and my four grandchildren. And what the calendar doesn't take care of, my wife happily does. It doesn't hurt that she's a firstborn and she loves to tell me what to do anyway, and I'm a baby of the family, so I'm used to being told what to do, where to go, and what time to be there. Do that nicely, like my wife does, and your husband will appreciate it too.

Sometimes you won't be able to celebrate a special event on the same day. My birthday is September 1, but this year I got my birthday card on October 4. On my actual birthday I was flying to New York to do a TV show. So my wife decided to surprise me by moving my birthday to October 4, complete with family party and gifts. It was classic Mrs. Uppington. My dear bride didn't want to simply tell me happy birthday on the phone; she wanted to celebrate me.

Focus on what's most important—that your wonderful spouse chose you to do life with.

## Haunted by First Sexual Experience

**Q:** I had sex for the first time when I was 15. I thought I was in love, but I was terribly wrong. My partner wanted nothing to do with me the next day or any day afterward. I was only another punch in his "man card." After that, I only wanted to get out of high school and away from that guy and all his friends, who thought I was someone they could use.

I met my husband in college. He was different—a guy I could trust and who believed in waiting for sex until marriage. We did great together until our honeymoon, when we had sex for the first time. I was really uncomfortable, and I know my husband noticed. I could see the disappointment in his eyes.

We've been married for two months now, and we've only attempted sex a couple more times. I could barely wait for it to be over. I love my husband, I think he's sexy, and I want to have sex with him. But I can't. What's wrong with me, and how can I fix it?

**A:** Clearly your first sexual experience was dreadful—scary and a disaster. You certainly don't have any positive feelings about it. Your first partner hurt you, used you, and betrayed you. First sexual experiences imprint themselves heavily on our minds because of the intense emotions involved, combined with the physical act of sex. Your memory of that event will always be there. But it doesn't have to overshadow your joy in the present with your husband—the man who loves you and cares about your well-being. I know that's easier said than done. However, unless you can forgive that boy in your past who used you and betrayed you, and call that experience what it was—a hormonal young man who only wanted you for sex, and you were needy enough to fall into that trap—you won't be able to move on. You were 15. You didn't know then what you know now.

It's important to separate your husband from that boy who used you. You said your husband is a man you can trust. In fact, that rock-solid man cared so much about you that he waited for sex, so your first time together would be in the safe boundaries of marriage. That says a lot about his character in our sex-saturated world.

You may also feel guilty that you couldn't give him what he gave you—his virginity. If so, now's the time to come clean if he doesn't know about your past. Yes, it will hurt, and you need to be prepared for his feelings of shock, anger, and betrayal, but it's information he needs to have so you can work through your reticence about sex together. Tell him that you wish you would have waited for sex. That you wish he was your first. That if you could go back and have a redo, you'd wait for him. Ask for his forgiveness for not waiting. Assure him that you desire him and find him sexy. That you ache to feel close to him and need his help in overcoming your memories.

Then celebrate by having some passionate sex where you focus on his face, so his image is emblazoned in your mind and connected to sexual play. Explore all of him and allow him to explore all of you. Practice often until your memories are filled with him and the intimacy you've experienced together. Then that hormonal boy who used you will recede into the distant past.

### Retired and Driving Me Crazy

**Q:** I love my man, but he's driving me crazy. He recently retired from a job he's had for nearly 40 years, and now he's home way too much. He spends his day following me around, telling me what I should do differently. I know murder's a capital crime, but it's becoming increasingly tempting. How can I get him to stay out of my business when he no longer has a business of his own? I want to send him away on a long vacation by himself.

**A:** Well, Arizona is nice this time of year, and it also has a lot of golf to keep him busy. Seriously, it sounds like your guy is having a hard time retiring and can't figure out what to do with himself. You've rowed your own canoe for a lot of years in managing the house and all those details, but now he's trying to take over the rowing, and it's driving you bonkers. Rightfully so. As a football coach's wife told me once, "I figured out why we got along so well—because my husband was always gone."

Now that you're in the same space 24/7, some role definition is in order. Have a meeting to decide who will take care of what. Draw up a checklist. If he wants you to shop at three stores instead of the one you go to in order to get the best bargains, then why shouldn't he do the grocery shopping? He'll discover fast enough it's not as easy as he thinks. Ditto with paying the bills. If you're stressed and have a lot on your platter, and he has the time, why shouldn't he ease your burden a little? However, it's important that you each have your own tasks, so he isn't redoing yours and frustrating you, and vice versa.

Men need to be needed by their wives. When they no longer have their life's work to keep them busy, they start to cast about, identity-less. If you don't allow him to make some of the daily tasks his to manage, he'll become a flaw picker who will drive you insane.

We're all creatures of habit. Retirement can be a time of great turmoil for a couple, or a time where a couple can kick back and enjoy doing things they've never had the opportunity or resources to do before. Encourage your spouse to pursue things he's interested in. Check out the community college for a class you might want to take together—social media, ballroom dancing, ceramics, or how to start your own business on the internet.

Most of all, relish those long sunsets, languid soaks in the tub, and leisurely lovemaking that you didn't have time for when the kids were underfoot. They'll make the retirement years exciting ones worth celebrating.

### How Much Sex Is Normal?

**Q:** I don't know how to ask this, but . . . how much sex is healthy, and how much is a problem—like sexual addiction? My husband is about to wear me out. We're two years into our marriage, and he acts like he's still on our honeymoon. He constantly needs sex. Every night, as soon as we finish our last bite of dinner, he's ready to head to the bedroom. I'm ready to do the dishes, put some sweats on, and take care of other house stuff. I wouldn't mind if he just wanted to snuggle, watch a movie, and maybe fondle a little, but he always wants the hot, sweaty kind where I'm exhausted afterward. Then I still have to do the dishes and anything else that needs to be done before morning. Worse, he expects me to want sex too, when he's ready for it.

What's normal for a guy who is 30 years old? I'm only four years older, but suddenly I'm feeling a lot older and pretty stressed too. Sometimes I just want time to paint my toenails or do something for myself, you know?

**A:** Some individuals have higher sex drives than others. It can be the husband or the wife. There's nothing wrong with having a high sex drive, as long as that spouse is sensitive, affectionate, and thoughtful toward his partner. Sometimes he should forgo his drive for sex and simply snuggle his partner.

But from what you said, I think you married a control freak. Yes, he may have a high sex drive, but if he expects you to always be ready when he is, then that's a control issue. He wants it when he wants it. And if he always craves the same kind of sex—hot and sweaty—then he also wants sex the way he wants it. He's not being considerate of you and your needs.

It's also possible he may be sexually addicted. Have you noticed him being drawn to sexually explicit images? Does he want to watch sex-laden movies? Does he quickly shut his laptop when you enter the room? If so, he may be drawn into the world of pornography. If he is, he will grow less sensitive to you and become even more forceful about pushing what he wants. People who are drawn to pornography see others as objects to be used rather than as spouses to love and relate to.

In your case, though, control seems to be the issue. He wants to know that he can control the sex part of your relationship—to get it when he wants it. Talk with your husband. Say, "Honey, sometimes I don't feel like having sex every night. I need to get other things done. Is there a reason you feel you need sex that often?" Tell him you want to have sex with him; it's important to you too. But you feel demeaned when he demands sex of you so often and at a specific time. Either he'll respect you and listen . . . or he won't. If he doesn't, try this experiment.

Go ahead and please him with sex when he wants it—after dinner. He'll think you've given in, that you're over your little tirade of words. Let him go to sleep thinking that. But then, sometime in the middle of the night, wake him up. Tell him you didn't get enough after dinner—that you want more sex right then and there. Take control and launch into the variety that he seems to like. Give it to him with gusto.

Do the same thing the next night—have sex after dinner, the way he wants it, and wake him up in the middle of the night for more. Yes, you'll be tired (take a nap if you can during the day), but aren't you tired anyway from the demands? Don't you want things to change?

Keep doing the experiment until you start to see some adjustments. If he's the controller I'm guessing he is, within a month he won't be able to get an erection. He won't be asking for sex after dinner every night. He'll want to snuggle and watch that movie sometimes. Then the two of you can figure out together how much sex each of you needs, and he'll be more respectful and considerate.

### Aging—Sex at a Standstill

**Q:** My husband's a healthy guy, with a usual sexual appetite. But when he hit his midfifties last year, we kinda hit a standstill. I'm eight years younger and am still craving sex with the man I love. He seems normal in every other way. Could it be me? He's less interested in me, or less interested in sex in general? Should I be concerned? Any ideas?

**A:** Hey, been there and done that. The years do take their toll. Mrs. Uppington and I are down to four or five times a week now, but we're dealing with it. Seriously, as men age, their testosterone levels and energy levels change. It happens to the best of us. As we get older, we have less energy. However, does that mean your sex life should stall? No. Gently tell your husband that you miss having sex with him, or having sex as frequently. Tell him you desire him and your feelings of wanting to be close to him haven't changed. Suggest that the two of you set up a doctor appointment for him to get the ol' plumbing checked out. Ask the doctor for suggestions based on the results, and decide together what options you're comfortable pursuing.

The most important thing is that the two of you are open with each other about how you're feeling. You may have to adapt your expectations as you come up with new ways to fit his current sexual drive with your craving for sex. Ask yourself, *Do I really want more sex? Or is it the intimacy of sex that I'm missing?* The answers to those questions will help you and your husband formulate a plan for moving forward.

The good news is, as we men age, we're more comfortable with cuddling and closeness—the two things women desire most. So use that to your advantage.

## I Have Two Babies—My Child and My Husband

**Q:** We had our first baby four months ago. With the lack of sleep and breast-feeding, I'm exhausted. I'm barely surviving here. I sleep like a baby—I'm up every two hours.

I dream of eating hot food for dinner. My husband goes to work during the day and comes home expecting everything to be like it was before we had the baby. Dinner on the table at six o'clock and a willing wife in bed. Now I'm lucky if I can cook a simple one-dish meal and don't have spit-up all over my T-shirt. I feel anything but sexy. But as soon as I get the baby down, my husband wants to get to other business, and sex is not on my mind. All I want to do is sleep when our daughter is sleeping.

My husband's getting grouchy. He says I don't have time for him anymore. But I don't know what else to do. I'm at the end of my energy level by the time I get the baby to bed.

**A:** Your husband is acting like a four-year-old who shaves. The world isn't all about him; it's about the three of you as a family. Of course you can't pay as much attention to him. You're the only one who can breast-feed that baby, but you're not the only one who can make dinner, do laundry, etc. Your husband is acting like a child instead of a man and needs to step up to the plate. You don't need a second baby. You need a real man who will stand by your side and do anything and everything, including changing diapers that require a hazmat suit.

170

Gently say to him, "Honey, I'd love to have some private time with you tonight. You know what I mean." Lift your eyebrows sensuously and smile. "But I'm starting to get really tired. If you could watch the baby and take care of the dishes while I shower, that would be great."

Then take an extra-long shower. Even a little time where he's all the way responsible for your baby should be an eye-opener. He can also learn to fold some laundry while he watches television. After all, his underwear and socks are in that basket too.

However, you're not off the hook. I know you're tired, and no wonder. But when that baby grows up and heads out the door, guess who will still be there? Your husband. That's why reserving some time and energy just for him is so important. So let those dust bunnies go. Take a nap when your baby does in the afternoon, to regain some of your energy.

Housework can wait. People need attention. Right now your baby will claim a lot of yours; she's helpless without you. But your husband also needs your attention. Streamline when you can. Serving macaroni and cheese on paper plates and asking friends, Grandma, and trusted babysitters for help are all doable and very good for upping your marital intimacy. Then your grouchy bear will be smiling like a cross-eyed Siamese cat and be willing to help you more, and your own stress level will go down and your sleep quotient will go up.

### Is My Spouse Having an Affair?

**Q:** My husband's sex drive has slowed way down. He also seems to have a lot of extra projects at work, where he has to stay late, and sometimes he misses dinner. I'm a little worried. What if he's having an affair?

**A:** A lot of men have times where their sex drive slows down for various reasons, including aging, career stress, or tension in the home. Your husband could simply be overstressed and tired from the extra workload. When the extra projects are done, he'll return to his normal sex drive.

Or, yes, something else could be going on. The first place to look is your relationship. Is your home a place of tension? Do you nag him about getting house repairs done when he walks in the door? Or do you welcome him with a kiss and open arms, even when he can't get everything done you'd like him to?

Another option is that your husband might be having an affair. If so, here are a few clues.

- When you say, "Oh, honey, tell me more about your project and how it's going," is he evasive? Does he give you details, or gloss over what he's doing or how long the project might last?
- When he misses dinner but says he's already eaten, say, "I hope you had something good. Would it help if I packed you extra food with your lunch so you could warm it up? Or maybe some nights I might be able to bring dinner to you so we could eat together." If he seems uncomfortable and won't tell you what he ate or where he got it, and he quickly says, "Oh, no, you don't need to come to the office," those are all red flags that need further investigation.
- He says he's meeting some people for dinner but doesn't give you their names. He only says, "Oh, they're just associates from work." If they are associates from work, he should be able to give you their first and last names.
- He has purchased new underwear or clothes recently, especially in a style he wouldn't typically wear.
- He has lost weight, is suddenly working to tone his muscles, and isn't going out of his way to flex those new biceps in front of you so you can admire them.

All those are simple clues that your spouse could be having an affair. If you do see any of those signs, be street smart. Check out the calls and texts on his cell phone, as well as his email messages and credit card charges. No, you shouldn't turn into a snoop, but women are very intuitive. If you have a gut feeling he might be having an affair, quietly follow through on some basic checkup. Just you, though—no calls to your girlfriends or your mother. Don't involve anyone else with your suspicions.

It's always better to know the truth than to wonder. And until you know, do not have sex with your husband. You certainly don't want to catch any disease that he might have contracted from a sexual partner who may have had multiple partners before him.

Perhaps the next time he calls to say he is working late and won't need dinner, stop by the office with some of his favorite takeout. If he isn't there, go back home. When he arrives home, don't interrogate him. Don't say right away that you paid him a visit and he was AWOL. Just say, "Wow, had to work late again, huh? That must be some project!" If he says, "Yeah, I worked until 6:30, and then Marty and I ran to Wendy's to grab a bite so we could go back and finish," you'll know he was likely working and you just missed him. But if he's evasive or doesn't mention he ran out to get a bite to eat, it's time to level with him. "You know, it's interesting. I was concerned you might be hungry, so I stopped by with your favorite takeout, and you weren't there. . . ."

If he isn't having an affair and he's simply overstressed and overworked, think of some solutions to his busyness. Are there things he regularly does at home that you could do for a while? And since everyone has to eat, could you pop in once a week and bring him dinner at the office? Even 15 minutes of eating takeout food together over his desk can help connect the two of you. And frankly, it sends a message to any female colleagues who might be hovering: *This man is definitely taken.*

### Romance Flew out the Window after "I Do"

**Q:** My dad's a romantic kind of guy. He kisses my mom every time he returns after being away from her, even if he's only going out to the garden shed. He brings her flowers spontaneously—no special occasion needed. When we were dating, my boyfriend was really romantic too. I loved that about him. I'd get flowers at least once a week, little notes under the windshield wipers on my car, and calls at work on my lunch hour.

Then we got married. Romance went out the window almost as soon as we said "I do." It's like as soon as we got married, some hidden switch was flipped. He started working really long hours, and romance was over. How can I get some of that old romance back?

**A:** Men can be so goal directed and driven that they drive right past you. Give your guy some credit, though. He believes he's making love to you by climbing the corporate ladder and working 12-plus hours a day. Most guys have one-track thinking, unless they're schooled otherwise. Your guy was competing to win the prize—you—and evidently he did a great job since he won your hand. Once you were married, he smiled and thought, *Hey, I got the marriage job done. Check. So, what should I go after next?* You see, healthy men are driven to accomplish what they set out to do. When he was dating, he pulled out all the stops to pursue you. He combed his hair, brushed his teeth, and even selected a shirt that wasn't from the rumpled stack on the floor beside his bed.

However, once he won you, his thoughts naturally moved to the next competition—whether that was building his career, saving for a home, etc. It doesn't mean he loves you any less; it's simply that he believes he accomplished the marriage job. He has secured you for a lifetime. If you think about it, that's actually a compliment! He knows he won your heart and is safe and secure in your love, so he can go on to his next challenge. That's what he's wired to do.

You, on the other hand, long for the little romantic gestures he used to do. You don't want to be the prize that's won only once. You want to know every day that you are special to him and that he thinks of you.

Since that guy of yours is clueless, as many guys are about romance, here's what I suggest. To get his undivided attention, touch him when you say, "Honey, I love you so much. I remember all the romantic things you've done for me. Every time you brought me a single flower, I felt special. I knew you'd picked me out of all the women in the world to love." Fluff up his manly feathers a little to get him on the same page with you. Then conclude with, "I know you're really busy right now with work, but I miss those little gestures. I'd love it if you did a few of them for me every once in a while."

Your guy will probably look shocked. "But, honey, you know I love you, right?" he says. "I told you that once, when I asked you to marry me, and nothing has changed." See what I mean? He thinks he got the marriage job done well and has been resting in the security of that. He's seen the best of you and the worst of you, and he still loves you. But if you explain to him that the little gestures are important reminders to you of his love, and that as a woman you need those, he'll get the picture.

One last thing. Your husband is not your dad. He's probably like him in many ways, because women often marry someone very much like their father. But you can't expect him to parrot what your dad does. Your husband is his own person, and the two of you have a unique relationship. Expecting him to be your dad, who is unusually romantic, will only lead to disappointment for you and frustration for him.

Let him be the man you married. He may not be the Don Juan he was when you were dating, but I know something for certain. After your gentle discussion, you better go get that flower vase ready. I'd bet you a Benjamin Franklin you'll get a delivery in the near future.

### He Wants Me to Initiate

**Q:** My husband says he'd really like me to initiate sex sometimes. I'm not comfortable with that. It's a little embarrassing. What if I initiate sex and he's not in the mood? Then what do I do? And why is it such a big deal to him that I'm the one who starts the process?

**A:** There are only four men in the continental United States and Canada who don't like the idea of the love of their life pursuing them. Most men just don't verbalize it. Good for your husband for telling you what he wants. It's hard enough for us guys to share our feelings and desires, much less to tell you something like that.

Every person carries around a sexual rulebook. We often don't know we have it until situations like this come up. Let me guess. You grew up in a conservative home where you were taught that the man should be the leader in all areas, including in romance and sex. In other words, men should chase women, not the other way around. Now your husband is basically asking you to chase him. You're uncomfortable with that because your husband is asking you to bend the "rule" you grew up with. But who says that rule is right? We all have rules, and we get them from the perceptions of life we form as we grow up.

I suggest that each of you take out the rulebooks you grew up with and examine them together. What do they say about the roles of men? The roles of women? As you study your rulebooks, you'll understand each other better and be able to brainstorm solutions you're both comfortable with.

Realize that anything you try for the first time will feel awkward. But if you love your husband, you'll affirm his masculinity by initiating sex sometimes. As for him not being in the mood? If you desire to please him and crook your little finger, I doubt you'll have any problem.

Men like both to do the chasing and to be chased. It makes us feel powerful and virile to experience both sides. Then we're like Tarzan in the bedroom, ready to do anything to please Jane. Let the jungle music begin.

### In the Mood More Than He Is

**Q:** We've been married for seven years, and we're in our early thirties. Our sex life is great . . . when we have it. The problem is that I'm in the mood a lot more than my husband is. When it comes to sex, he's a two-times-a-month guy. I'd like it at least four times a week. I guess I always thought men wanted sex more than women, so am I weird? Or is there something wrong with him? And what should I do if I'm in the mood and he's not? I go to bed frustrated a lot of nights.

**A:** Each spouse has a varying energy level, a different sex drive, and a rulebook they grew up with. Part of growing together is discovering how those three things affect your intimacy and sex life. As both of you mature in your relationship, you should also become more willing to change your behavior because you realize what's important to your spouse. For example, since your husband's sex drive is lower than yours and you're going to bed frustrated, you need to be honest with him. "Honey, I crave sex with you. And not just twice a month. I'm in the mood at least four times a week. Any ideas for how we could handle that difference?" Men are problem solvers at their core, and since you've just given him a problem to solve, he'll be busily on it.

You can also try the technique of anticipation. It works wonders for the male species. Prepare him in advance for the evening you'd like to have. Grab him by the tie and give him a thorough kiss in the morning as he's heading out the door. Tell him, "That's just a taste of what you're going to get when you come home."

You'll have that man salivating all day and Mr. Happy more than ready for a romp. Setting the mood with a few candles, some food you can feed each other, wearing an outfit that catches his attention, and touching him can also up your romance and sex quotient.

The point is, both of you need to figure out what works. But since you're the one who is craving more sex, you'll need to encourage it to happen.

## He Falls Asleep Right after Sex

**Q:** Right after we have sex, my husband rolls over and goes to sleep on his side of the bed. Job done. For him, at least. But I'm frustrated. I want more. More stroking, more cuddling. I want to fall asleep in his arms. Frankly, I don't need the sex, but I do need the intimacy. Am I weird?

**A:** No, you're not weird. Women long for a heart connection. They want to know that they are loved in a way that doesn't lead to baby making. They need to feel intimate emotionally before they can be intimate physically. And even when intercourse is complete, they desire a continuation of that emotional connection. For most women, stroking and cuddling is far more romantic than the act of sex itself. They want soul partners, not merely bed partners.

Your husband, however, isn't a woman. He doesn't innately know or understand a woman's needs. He's a guy, and he thinks his job is done ... and done well, I might add. That's why he's bedded down next to you like a contented, hibernating bear.

What does your guy need? A little guidance as to what he should do to please you. Who can he best get that from? You. Hints won't do it. Plain speaking is best. "Honey, after we make love, it's very important to me that we snuggle. I need to continue feeling close to you. Would you just hold me in your arms?"

That man will happily oblige you. He likes feeling your skin next to his too. Then, even if he does fall asleep, you're encircled by the warmth of his arms and you get the closeness you long for. You might even fall asleep yourself.

## Couch-Potato Husband

**Q:** I'm starved for attention from my couch-potato husband. I've lost a lot of weight recently and am looking better than I have in years. In fact, a co-worker has been giving me a lot of compliments recently. He seems to notice everything. When I was shopping for a dress, I caught myself thinking, *I wonder what Frank would think.*

Frank's my co-worker, not my husband. That scared me a little. I remember what you said about it being easy to fall into an affair, and I don't want to be that kind of woman. My husband is still the man I want to be married to, but I need him to notice things like when I get a new dress or change my hairstyle. But I don't think he'd notice even if I came in with a bag over my head. How can I drag his focus away from what feels like his girlfriend—the television?

**A:** Good for you for being honest about your vulnerability. If things don't change quickly, you will end up in your co-worker's arms. The average marriage lasts a whopping seven years. You don't want to be one of the statistics. That couch-potato husband of yours needs a wake-up call, and the sooner, the better.

Walk straight into the TV room, take that treasured remote control, and flip off the TV. Tell him, "Honey, I love you, but it's important that we talk, and it can't wait. I've worked really hard to look good for you, and you don't even seem to notice. The only important thing in your life seems to be work . . . and television. I'm dying for some attention here. In fact, I'm so starved for it that when a male co-worker compliments me, he's starting to look good to me."

That ought to make your guy sit straight up on the couch.

For the normal, average couch-potato husband, there's nothing like the shock of some potential competition to kick his interest in pursuing you into high gear. And as he does, he'll start to view you again as the desirable, sexy woman you truly are. Then sexual intimacy and all the loving attention you deserve will be back as featured items on the marital menu.

Bon appétit!

## Struggling with Intimacy

**Q:** For five years of my childhood I was sexually abused by my stepfather and stepbrother. When my mother found out, she kicked them both out. But the damage was already done. I didn't date much in high school because I felt used and dirty, and I couldn't trust men. It's a miracle I fell in love with my husband, who was a co-worker for several years before I agreed to date him. He was the first guy I learned to trust.

Since we got married a year ago, though, I've struggled to give myself to him. Every time we have sex, flashes of my childhood abuse enter my mind. The very idea of sex with anyone is sickening to me. All I want is to get the sex over with, so just like on the nights where I was abused, I imagine I'm somewhere else—like a warm, sandy beach, where I'm alone and safe. I know my husband loves me, but I don't feel loved when we have sex. I feel used once again. I really, really love my husband and want to please him, but I'm secretly terrified to give of myself in that way again. Can you help me? Help us?

**A:** What happened to you in your childhood was the result of men who exerted their craving for control in a terrible way. No wonder you struggle with the concept of sex, because to you, sex does not equal love. It means a male dominating a female, as your stepfather and stepbrother did to you. As much as you trust your husband, he is still a man, and your traumatic past will make you fight against being dominated by a male.

First, you need to not only know in your head but also take into your heart the fact that the abuse was not your fault. In no way did you cause it. You were an innocent child. Men who use women and girls in such a way are sick and perverted. They often have been sexually abused themselves in childhood and don't have the coping skills to break the chain of abuse.

You too have been betrayed by family members you should have been able to trust. Recovering and reclaiming your sexuality after sexual abuse is a time-consuming and emotionally exhausting process. You can't do it alone.

And I have to ask: does your husband know you were sexually abused? If not, it's time to tell him. Don't wait for fear of what he'll say. That guy you love deserves to know about all of you—and that includes the details of your past that you hate to remember. Chances are, he will at first be intensely angry at the men who were so sick and twisted they abused a child in such a way. But that doesn't mean he's angry at you. Your husband wants to be your lover, yes. But he also wants to be your protector, your hero. That strong man will likely gather you in his arms and cry with you because you had to suffer such horrible events.

Let him know what you need. "Honey, it's so hard for me to tell you this and talk about it. Would you just hold me?"

If you don't tell him, that wonderful man may think you are rejecting him instead of realizing that you struggle with male domination and sexual intimacy as a result of your experiences.

When he knows why you are reticent about having sex—that it scares you—you can talk together about ways to adapt your approach to give you more control of the situation.

Here are some suggestions that will help.

You may feel more comfortable being in the driver's seat—for example, on top of your husband during foreplay and sex, rather than him covering you. That way you're not in the same position as when you were dominated by your stepfather and stepbrother, who took advantage of you.

If certain areas of the house, such as bedrooms, spark memories of the abuse, pursue sexual experiences with your husband elsewhere. Set up a romantic mood. Add candles, drag a mattress into the sunroom, and have sex there with the warm, bright sunshine beaming in on you. Don't wait until nighttime, prompting memories of men abusing you in the dark.

Take the lovemaking slowly, with lots of cuddling and stroking and whispered words of love so you feel cherished and safe and comfortable before your husband penetrates you. Focus on the warmth and the cuddling—things you didn't get when you were violated and that you deeply desire in the relationship with your husband. Steer clear of any acts you were forced to do with your stepfather and stepbrother. Instead, your husband should focus on pleasing you—whatever feels good and you're comfortable with.

There is a wonderful book by Dan Allender called *The Wounded Heart: Hope for Adult Victims of Childhood Sexual Abuse* that may be a great help to you. I've recommended it for years and have seen the significant impact of its message of hope and healing on countless people who have experienced childhood sexual abuse and continue to deal with the aftermath of it.

With such trauma in your past, I suggest you and your husband go to counseling together. After all, you're in this marriage together. What affects one of you affects the other. That man who loves you will be happy to go with you. The sooner you get help from a professional, the better.

If you approach the situation as a challenge to handle as a couple rather than as "your problem," you can find new ways to engage in marital intimacy. You two deserve to reap the lifetime rewards of a healthy, fun sex life and the warmth of marital intimacy. Together you can get there.

## He Lost His Job . . . and His Sex Drive

**Q:** My husband lost his sex drive eight months ago—right after he lost his job. At first he hunted crazily for another job. But now he just sits around. He can't seem to pull it together. I try to initiate sex, but he shows no interest. How can I prove to him that he's still my man—job or no job? And that I still desire him physically?

**A:** A man is driven to compete, and part of that competition is providing financially for his family. Right now your husband feels like a failure. Mr. Happy isn't going to get happy when your husband is in the mode of thinking he's failed you and your family. What does he need most?

You're already on the right track. He needs to know he is still valued and respected in your eyes—job or no job. Look for situations where he can problem-solve for you. Women really don't want their husbands to solve problems; they want their husbands to know what they're up against. However, in this situation, it's important for you to tune in to his need to contribute to the family. He needs to know you need him. So create situations where you can say, "Honey, I need your help with something. I know you can help me because you're so good at looking at problems from all angles. Here's the situation. . . ."

You are sharing your heart and problems with the man you love, and here's what he's thinking as a result: *Wow, the woman I love needs me. Sure, I lost my job, but that doesn't mean I'm good for nothing. I'm good for something. I'm needed in her life . . . in my family's life.* Such positive thinking will spur your man on to find the perfect job. He may receive rejection in that job hunt, but he knows he will come home to a wife who loves him, needs him, and respects him.

He also needs to know that you still desire him as much as you did before—that losing his job didn't make him less of a man in your eyes. He certainly doesn't need any pressure about job hunting, nor does he need you pestering him for sex. What he does need is the physiological release that sex can bring, as well as the relational connection it fosters in your marriage. But in his discouragement, he may not have the drive he usually has to pursue sex himself.

Here's what I suggest. If you have kids, arrange to send them to Grandma's house or a neighbor's tonight for a couple of hours. Tell that man of yours you've planned a special time just for the two of you, and give him a smile and a suggestive wink. Let him anticipate that time all day.

After the two of you enjoy your intimate evening, I bet he'll have more swagger in his step the next day. He might even go back to job hunting without you nagging. That's because the person who means the most to him is you. The person he wants to please the most is you. And when you reserve some time and energy for him and show your pleasure in what he can still do for you and to you, you're giving him his masculinity back.

## Too Flabby for Sex

**Q:** I'm not in the same shape I was in before I had the baby—not even close. I'm working on it, but the extra flab won't go away. My husband still tries to get me in bed when the baby's asleep, but I find myself making lots of excuses. I look in the mirror and don't like the way my belly and breasts look, so how could he? Yet how do I hold him off until I get back into shape? How long should we wait?

**A:** There's this new invention called a baby stroller. After your hubby goes to work, or after you get home from work, put that little baby—your precious gift—in that stroller. Go for a walk.

"Leman," you say, "I live in Minnesota. Are you crazy? I can't do that kind of thing year-round."

No, I'm not crazy. If I remember right, you live where the biggest mall in the entire United States is—the Mall of America. Go to the mall, set up your baby in the stroller, and walk. Your baby will be fascinated by the constantly changing parade, and you'll get some exercise in.

Even better, load up that baby in the morning and take a brisk walk with your husband before one or both of you head off to work, and then take another together right before dinner. You both get physical exercise that way.

I know you're tired. But exercise has a wonderful result—more energy. Walking also would give you and your spouse a chance to organize your day as it's getting started and then to debrief at the end of it. And that baby of yours who might otherwise be crying as you're trying to talk is quietly enjoying a whole panorama of scenes, including the dog next door and the neighbor's baby who just went by in her stroller. Walking together is a wonderful way to get on the same page with the person you love and remain there.

Pregnancy is a stressful time in a marriage, and so is birthing a baby and the recovery period. How long should you wait to have sex after having a baby? The standard answer is six to eight weeks, but you should let your doctor tell you. Even better, have your husband come to the appointment with you so he hears the answer for himself about how you're doing.

For many couples, though, it takes a lot longer before their sex life gets back on track. The wife needs time to physically recover and often lives on the edge of exhaustion. At the same time she's not at the top of her game physically or emotionally, she's meeting the nonstop needs of a new little human being, and her husband is giving her the fish eye.

Truth is, after you've had a baby your body will never quite look the same. That might bother you, but it doesn't seem to bother your husband. He still desires you. So why should you hold back? In fact, your breasts might be fuller since the baby, so why shouldn't he have fun with them? When you can't enjoy sex with him because you've got a few extra pounds, that's like sticking a dagger in his heart. You're shooting him and his masculinity down.

But it doesn't have to be that way. Do you know what the sexiest thing you can have is? A positive attitude. So tell that man, "I'm feeling a little fat and self-conscious right now, but I know you'll accept me just the way I am. I need you in my life. I want you." Open your arms to him. Your words and your willingness will drive him to a new desire to please you in as many different ways as he can. He won't even notice you're not the same size.

### Can We Just Cuddle?

**Q:** Sometimes all I want is to cuddle or snuggle. Or even to get a back rub after a long day. But to my husband, any touching has to lead somewhere, and that somewhere is sex. Is that a male thing? How can I get him to understand that just because I want to be close or sit next to him, it isn't a signal that I want sex?

**A:** Most women prefer the closeness and cuddling of marital intimacy rather than the act of sex itself. In fact, they'd rather give up the rush of orgasm for snuggling. Men are programmed to want sex. One look at you in a clingy outfit, and he'll pay attention. But he also wants more than anything else to please you.

We men are straightforward critters. Tell us what to do, and we'll do it. If you only want to snuggle and don't want things to progress to more, say, "Hon, I'm really tired and a bit overwhelmed with all I have to do. I'd love it if you would just put your arm around me as we sit on the couch. I need your strength tonight." What are you saying in a nice way? "No hanky panky tonight, mister, but I still need your strength and feel better when your arm is around me." So even though you're temporarily shutting off the sex, you're still stroking that male ego by stating you value his strength and need him in your life.

## Dying for Some Romance

**Q:** We have two kids under the age of three. I'll be blunt. Any romance we had went the way of the dodo bird when children came along. I'd love for my husband to surprise me and spirit me away to our bedroom for a romantic rendezvous during nap-time—or anytime—but he's never in the mood. It's like as soon as I had the babies, I'm now "mom" to him instead of wife and lover. How can I get him past the "we have kids now" thinking, so he becomes more than just a warm body next to me in bed? I'm dying for some romance here.

**A:** How much sex a couple has—or doesn't have—is a good barometer for how their marriage is doing. If you are empty, alone, and without romance, then your marriage needs paddles to get it started at its heart again. Yes, you're busy, but there's more going on than that. In a healthy marriage, difficulties drive you closer together. But if there's a conflict between the two of you, that can drive you apart. Your feelings are a wake-up call for something in your relationship that needs to be addressed. Feelings can draw you together to make your marriage hum, but judgments—assuming you know how and why your husband is doing what he's doing—will drive you apart.

Look at the situation for an instant from your husband's point of view. Is he feeling overwhelmed by being a daddy now? Trying to figure out how to juggle work and time with the kids? Is he anxious about the extra financial burden that having two kids adds and wondering if his job pays enough or if he should look for something else too? Does he crave physical intimacy with you but doesn't know how to ask since he sees that you're tired and really busy with the kids? These are all very good possibilities.

But let me also be clear here. You are not his mama. You are his wife. If he's confusing the two, you need to kindly set the record straight. He might need to call you "Mom" in front of your two little darlings, but he should not address you that way when it's just the two of you.

You and your husband need to set up an intimate dinner minus kids, some face-to-face discussion, and some naked skin time. It's amazing what even one evening like that can accomplish in getting you both back on track.

# *Tuesday*

## *Why Men Want Sex*

What men need the most, what they want the most, and why they need foreplay just as much as women do.

### Sex Is a Distant, Pleasant Dream

**Q:** My wife and I have four boys. They're stair steps and fight all the time. My wife jokes that they have to be watched so they don't kill each other. I sometimes wonder if she's right. We pray for the day the first one goes to all-day kindergarten, because it'll seem like a vacation. Is that so wrong?

Sex is a distant, pleasant dream. We know we had it, since we have the kids as living proof. But now, in the midst of a chaotic houseful, how are my wife and I supposed to carve out time for ourselves? Especially when we're not rolling in cash to get babysitters?

**A:** It's time to get creative. You two need and deserve some planned vacations from your four playful otters—though I'm sure they're adorable otters 1 percent of the time. Your wife needs to eat somewhere that doesn't serve Kool-Aid and pizza, and you both need to have some couple time, outside of the demands of those four little boys.

You mentioned money issues. There's a wonderful concept called *bartering*. Switch babysitting with another couple. You take their kids for an evening, then they take yours for an evening (and blessings upon them with four boys!). Each couple gets a rare treat—to enjoy a free evening with no kids. Yes, the night with the other kids might be crazy, but isn't life that way already? Adding a few extra kids might take your boys' attention away from killing each other and give you a break. And just think of all the wonderful things you can do with your spouse on the night you don't have your kids. That ought to bring a smile.

Competent high school babysitters you know well can also work wonders in giving you a breather. Teenagers usually have a lot more energy than you do by evening or on a Saturday. Try a little bartering there too. What do they need that you or your wife can supply? Homemade goodies or a decorated cake for a party? A car for a special event? A garage for a Friday night rehearsal with their musically inclined friends? Some help tie-dyeing T-shirts to give their friends because you know how to and they don't?

Being strapped for cash doesn't mean you can't make couple time a priority. Do little things that will reap big rewards with the woman you love. Take the kids to an outdoor park. Let them play, scream, and wear themselves out. You take a nice leisurely walk around the playground and hold your wife's hand like you used to when you were dating. When those boys are exhausted, drive home and tuck them in bed. Then you and your wife are free to do some calisthenics all your own.

You'll also be amazed how far a few bucks can go when you get creative. Set aside 10 bucks a week for couple time. Bet you can think of a zillion ways to spend it. Most of all, have fun.

## Starving for Physical Affection

**Q:** My wife has never been comfortable with physical touch. Nobody in her family is a hugger. In my family, everybody hugs, and they do it often. I can't remember a day when I was a kid that my parents didn't hug me. When I walk in the door now, all I want is a hug, a kiss, and a "Welcome home." Okay, I admit, I want a lot more sex too. Every time I broach the subject, though, my wife bristles. "Well, your family is different from mine," she says. "I didn't grow up like that." How can I tell my wife I'm starving for some affection?

**A:** Women are naturally relational creatures who love to hug and be hugged. If your wife isn't, chances are that either she grew up in a home where touching was considered inappropriate, or she was inappropriately touched by someone in her family or extended family, so she always has her guard up. It's important to gently get at the root of why she isn't comfortable with physical affection. Yes, your families are different, but why are they different? What in your wife's growing-up years led her to feel uncomfortable with such exchanges?

Also, it has been said that opposites attract. That is clearly the case with the two of you. What attracted you to your wife in the first place? Was it because the two of you were so different, and you were fascinated by those differences? Has she always been like this—edgy about affection—and you just recently noticed? If so, wow, you must have been wearing the "I'm in love" blinders, because your relational styles are poles apart.

It will take a lot of hard work to bring your two personalities and backgrounds together to make your marriage into an orchestra that can perform a lifelong concerto.

We men are simple and have three basic needs: to be wanted, to be needed, and to be respected. If a wife respects her husband, she will meet his needs, including his sexual needs. There's nothing that downs a husband's self-worth faster than a wife who reluctantly hugs, kisses, or has sex with him. It creates resentment on both their parts. Too many couples settle for the husband begging for biological release and the wife grudgingly accommodating him. But that's not emotionally fulfilling for either partner, nor does it create the marital intimacy both long for.

Strange as this may sound, great sex doesn't come naturally. It's not merely a biological function; it has a highly emotional component that requires a connection of hearts and desire. You have to work to become a better lover. That means you spend time thinking of ways to keep sex fresh and to help your reticent spouse discover what would satisfy her sexually and thus make her eager to be intimate with you.

So talk to your wife. Tell her that hugs, kisses, and a "Welcome home" are really important to you. Say that you desire her physically and that without sex, you feel rejected and empty. "Honey," you add, "if there is anything I can do differently to make you feel more comfortable with sex, I sure would like to know."

Then shut your mouth and prepare to listen. You may not like what you hear, because there may be things about her life growing up that shock you but will explain her reticent behavior. She may also fire back an onslaught of things that would make her feel loved but that you aren't doing. No matter what she has to say, you need to hear it. Your relationship can't change without both of you truth-speaking in love.

Whatever your wife has to say is much better than the alternative—her blowing off such a conversation and refusing to talk about it. If she does, it's time to get a counselor involved. Because of the type of family you grew up in, unless you receive physical intimacy soon from your wife, you're an easy target for an affair. If you can't go to your spouse for your basic needs to be met, your emptiness and loneliness might tempt you to seek comfort from someone outside your marriage.

You can't let this one slide. There's far too much at stake. So get to the root of her reticence, and then form a workable plan together for growing in marital intimacy.

## What Happens in the Bedroom . . . Stays in the Bedroom

**Q:** I just found out that my wife's best friend knows an awful lot about our sex life, and I'm not comfortable with that. Frankly, I'm embarrassed. To me, sex is private, something that should happen between the two of us and only be discussed between the two of us. My wife loves to talk. She shares everything with her best girlfriend. But I don't want our sex life to be part of their gossip. How can I explain that to my wife? She doesn't seem to think there's anything wrong with it.

**A:** No wonder you're uncomfortable. Your wife talking to her friend about your sex life is a violation of your marriage vows. It would be like you broadcasting to the guys you work with what your wife's breast size is or how much she weighs. I doubt she'd want those details spread around.

You need to gently say to your wife, "Honey, I know that you talk to So-and-So about what happens in our bedroom. But I'd like what happens between you and me to stay between you and me. If you have anything to say about it, I want to be the first and only one to hear it." Honestly, that's where discussion of your sexual experiences should stay—between the two of you—unless you're in counseling together with a third party who is helping you with that aspect of your marriage.

## She Had a Hysterectomy

**Q:** Everything in our sex life changed after my wife had a hysterectomy. She seems less interested in sex, and everything I've done in the past 30 years doesn't work anymore. I'm floundering in the wilderness with no direction. Any ideas?

**A:** Of course things have changed. Your wife may be feeling less feminine because she's missing some of her female body parts. Women who go through mastectomies often feel the same way. Assure your wife that she is just as beautiful and sexy to you as she always has been, even with a few scars and some internal parts MIA. Also, because those parts are missing, she may need to be stimulated differently in foreplay.

What's most important is communication. When you begin lovemaking, ask her what feels good and realize that what feels good will change from time to time—she's not only aging, but she's had surgery. Ask her to guide your hands, your lips, and other body parts to where she wants them to go. Tell her you want to please her. Right now she's functioning like a slow cooker, a little slow to warm up. But the right words will turn her into a microwave. Who knows? She might be pursuing your own body shortly.

## Had Sex with Others before We Met

**Q:** When I was in high school, a lot of my football teammates used girls for what they could get out of them, then walked away. I wasn't that kind of guy, and my mom had drilled staying a virgin into my head. As a sophomore, I dated a freshman for three months. One night things got out of control, and we ended up going all the way. I couldn't look at her the same way after that, and every time we were together we fell into more sex. I felt guilty because I knew I wasn't going to marry her, so I finally broke up with her. She was crushed. To this day I still feel terrible for how I treated that girl. She deserved better.

Neither my wife nor I discussed whether we were virgins before we got married. Afterward I found out she'd had sex in high school. At first I was really angry, because I wish she'd told me the truth before we got married. Then again, I didn't tell her I wasn't a virgin either. I still haven't. I guess both of us thought that what was in the past should stay in the past. Now I'm sad. Somebody used my wife-to-be just like I used that girl. We can't wipe the past away, and it's put a major kink in our sex life. Where do we go from here?

**A:** You need to be honest with each other. Don't give specifics, because you don't need any more pictures in your mind than are already there. However, you should tell your wife that you dated a girl in high school and that you didn't treat her well. To this day it bothers you.

Say to your wife, "She deserved better. When I found out some guy did that to you, I was really angry at him. Then I felt sick, because I realized I had done the same thing. It made me scared and sad, and I thought, *I don't deserve you.* I wish I could wipe away the past for both of us so that we were both virgins. But I know that can't happen."

Then look her straight in the eye when you say, "Honey, you deserve better than a guy like me. In fact, I can't believe you chose to marry me. I want to spend the rest of my life loving you and getting to know you better. In my eyes you are pure, and you didn't deserve what happened to you. I want to make you a vow that I will never break. I vow to never use and abuse you like I did that girl, or like that guy did you. Can we start from here and go forward?"

You will still have some stones in the path because of those past experiences, but at least now you can move forward, with no secrets dividing you.

### Painful Sex—Real or in Her Head?

**Q:** Having sex for us as a couple has always been hard. From the very beginning my wife has said it hurts every time I enter her. I guess I thought sex was just supposed to happen—a natural thing—between two people who loved each other. But we barely have sex. When we do, she cries, and she's really sore afterward. Doc, I have to know. Is this in her head, or does it really hurt her physically? If so, what am I doing wrong? I don't want to hurt my wife, but I'm dying for a little action.

**A:** Many women have pain with intercourse for a wide range of reasons. It's possible that neither of you is doing anything wrong but that sex is painful for her. If there's vaginal pain, now is the time to explore the causes of it and to pursue treatment. You don't want the idea of sex paired with pain imprinted in your wife's brain.

Book an appointment with her gynecologist, and go to the appointment together. Explain that you're having difficulty with sex because it's painful for your wife. Your wife should go through a physical exam.

It's possible your wife is experiencing vaginismus, where the pain happens only with penetration—where she feels like something is being torn inside or the penis is hitting a wall. Vaginismus is often linked to the anxiety or fear of having sex and can come as a result of childhood abuse, rape, or growing up in a home where talk about sex was forbidden. Loving, gentle foreplay, and plenty of it, is especially important in helping your wife relax.

She might have a tipped uterus and/or a short cervix. If so, then certain sexual positions will be more comfortable to her, such as her being on top. Guiding your penis inside at an angle she can control and using lubricants will ease the entry.

If your wife is petite, she could have a narrow passageway, and your penis may be a lot larger than the average male's.

These are only a few of the possibilities, but the gynecologist will be able to provide other information and offer solutions. The important thing is that you find answers together. It's not just her problem; it's your challenge as a couple. Don't miss out on the incredible intimacy of sex. Find ways that work.

## Our Sizzle Has Fizzled

**Q:** We've been married for over 20 years, and things in the sex department are pretty dull. My wife used to really turn me on, and I still find her body interesting, but I don't feel the sizzle I used to. I've tried to resurrect those early-marriage "gotta have sex or I can't stand it" feelings, but I can't. Is that normal for married couples once they reach the second decade? Am I just hoping for something that won't happen? Or should I accept things the way they are?

**A:** Move over and make room right next to you, because thousands of other men and women are asking the same question. I bet you thought when you got married, *Wow, look at that. I've got a hot woman in my bed. I get to have sex as much as I want now. What's not to love about that?*

Then real life entered—the nine-to-five annoyances called jobs, mortgage payments, and leaky faucets. Then you had a couple of those . . . what do you call them? . . . yes, children. And your mother-in-law? Not getting along with her put a dent in your sex life too.

But there's something else I want you to notice in the way you penned your question. See the "I" in your statements? Could you be focused a little too much on yourself and not your wife? What about her needs?

What do women want? To be held, to be listened to, to be cuddled. They want a flower . . . even when it's not their birthday or a Hallmark-marketed holiday. Your wife's purpose in life isn't to fulfill all your needs for pleasure. She's supposed to be your soul mate too.

What if, instead of focusing on the sizzle and sex you're not getting, you shine the spotlight on your wife and her needs? Listen to her, help her around the house, do little things that show how much you love her. As you focus on who she is, she'll become even more beautiful to you . . . yes, even after 20 years. Make a list of all the wonderful reasons you married her, and share one reason with her each day.

As you do these things, giving of yourself instead of only expecting her to give to you, your emotions will change. Mr. Happy may not always stand up and pay attention, and you may not have those early-marriage feelings all the time, but you'll be growing something that lasts a lifetime—a mature love that will overcome any and all obstacles. Marriage is about finding out what each of you needs, giving that to each other, and humbly serving each other.

There's a bonus too. When you show your wife how precious she is to you in small ways, the resulting sizzle in the bedroom might rival anything you've ever had and more.

## Do Birth Control Pills Lower Sex Drive?

**Q:** My wife and I were both virgins when we went on our honeymoon. We waited a long time for sex, but I was disappointed with the way she responded. I expected a volcanic eruption or the heights of Mount Everest, but it was more like a momentary blip on a computer screen. She just didn't seem that interested in sex or in exploring my body, even though I was very interested in hers.

I read something online about birth control pills dampening a woman's sex drive. Is that true? She's on the pill because we're not yet ready to start a family. We've only been married six months. But if it is the pill, I think we need to try something different, because I really want a wife who desires and enjoys sex. Advice?

**A:** Birth control pills can lower sex drive in some women. However, there are many formulas for birth control pills. Go back to the gynecologist, explain what's happening, and see if he or she can prescribe other possibilities. Also discuss other options, such as condoms, diaphragms, IUDs, and natural family planning methods to see if any of these might work better for you.

You know all those commercials about men who have low "T" and need Viagra? Well, Viagra for a woman is holding her tenderly, listening, communicating, sharing your feelings, and telling her how precious she is to you. Before you change birth control pills, give those methods a try first.

## I Love Her Naked, But She Says She's Fat

**Q:** I love to look at my wife's naked body, but she hates to be seen naked. She says she's fat, so she turns the lights out and then gets into bed quickly and pulls the sheets up to her chin. I like snuggling her that way before we have sex, but what I'd really love is to see her get undressed . . . or, even better, help her get undressed. Seeing her strip naked, like she did on our honeymoon, turns me on. She's a gorgeous woman, and she's mine. But it seems she's always patting her stomach and thighs and saying she needs to work off some of the pounds. Honestly, who cares about the extra pounds? We've been married for 12 years, and I've got some too, from her good cooking. How can I help her understand that, to me, she's as sexy as the day I married her?

**A:** You're a red-blooded male, and you get turned on by looking. That's natural. Tell her the things you told me—that she's gorgeous and seeing her naked turns you on. Stroke her all over with her clothes on. Ask her if, as a present to you, she'd allow you to "unwrap" her and feast your eyes on her before you get into bed.

If her old nighties don't fit, spirit her away for a shopping trip sometime for some new ones . . . just her size. Whisper sweet somethings in her ear. Tell her how sexy and beautiful she is. Many women struggle with insecurity about their weight, so she's not alone. But if you show her with your gentle, loving touch that the pounds don't matter, as well as tell her, that woman will become a tiger in your bed.


## Drawn to Porn

**Q:** I'm a very visual guy. Every day on my way home from work, I drive by signs for a strip club and a XXX-rated movie store. I have to admit, I've looked at some pornography online during my breaks at work. I love my wife, but somehow I can't stop wanting to look. What's wrong with me, and how can I fix it?

**A:** First of all, let your boss discover porn on your computer, and that's a great way to end your career. Is your little sneak peek during breaks really worth that possibility?

The reality is, guys are visual, and they are drawn by sexual images. You have a choice to make. How pure do you want to be so you can focus your attention on that lovely wife of yours without having other images intrude? If you continue down the track of viewing pornography, it will be even harder to stop. Pornography is a very destructive force on relationships because it turns people into objects to be used. Think of a hurricane wind blowing through your marriage, wreaking havoc and tearing down your house, and you've got it. That's why you have to stop now.

To decrease the lure of pornography in your life, here are some suggestions:

- Take a different route home, even if it uses more gas and takes more time.
- Focus your sexual thoughts on your wife and on providing her pleasure to combat the impure images of pornography and the insidious view of women as objects of lust.
- When you access the internet at work, angle your computer screen so that anyone walking by can see it. Then you'll be less tempted to access porn sites. Do the same thing when you're at home. Work in the kitchen or with your wife sitting next to you on the couch.
- Identify the times you're tempted and the triggers that draw you toward pornography. Do you not know what to do with yourself on that 15-minute break at work? Are you trying to avoid a boring task at home? Did you have a disagreement with your wife? Do you struggle with not enough sex or unsatisfying sex in your marriage? After you pinpoint the time frames and the triggers for temptation, take steps to address those specific issues.

  For many guys, boredom is a trigger, and they need to find an alternative to turning on the computer. But men aren't the only ones who view pornography. For women, the reason typically is loneliness—a lack of relationship. Phoning a friend, meeting a colleague for lunch, or taking a walk in the park with a family member is a healthier alternative to surfing porn on the internet.
- Find people who can relate to your struggle but will check in with you and hold you accountable to stay away from pornography.

One of the lures of pornography is its secretive nature. Remove the mystery and the secret, and pornographic images will tempt you less. You'll still be tested, but as you use the suggestions above, over time pornography will have less of a foothold in your life.

## Searching for That Elusive Climax

**Q:** My wife isn't able to climax by me entering her. She needs to be rubbed and touched before I enter her. Is that normal? I thought the best sex is being able to climax together, when I'm inside her. What am I missing?

**A:** Actually, it's normal for a woman to need stroking and direct stimulation of her clitoris to reach orgasm. Only a third of women can reach orgasm through intercourse. Your wife is in the healthy two-thirds of the population. So add a lot of foreplay to your sexual intimacy, and you'll both soar to new and exciting heights.

## We Can't Get Pregnant

**Q:** For three years we've been trying to conceive a baby, with no luck. I'm ready to give up and pursue adoption. To me, a baby is a baby, no matter where that child comes from. But my wife is driven to feel what it's like to carry a child. To her, sex is all about getting that baby. There's no pleasure or excitement in it anymore. I just get a phone call to "hurry home because it's time" when she's ovulating. Sometimes I can't drum up the enthusiasm, because there's no passion anymore.

I'm tired of hearing about her temperature, where she is in her cycle, and how we should position ourselves in sex to get a boy or girl. What's even worse is all the crying every month when she finds out she's not pregnant. I really want to be more to my wife than a sperm donation. But right now that's all I feel like. I still love her, but I'm starting to not like her. There's only so much a man can take. Help?

**A:** You need to have a candlelit dinner, get naked in the tub together, and have a heart-to-heart. Tell her how much you love her. Explain that you'd love to have a baby with her, but it's not happening. Share with her that sex has become rote—something you have to do on a schedule—and it's not satisfying for you that way. Yes, she'll cry, but she's been crying a lot anyway, hasn't she? So buck up, be the husband she needs you to be, and tell the truth gently about how you feel.

Now's the time to ask her, sensitively, why it's so important to her to carry a child within her body. Then get together with your doctor and discuss other options. Look at the success rates and your finances, and then the two of you will need to make some decisions. If you do have that baby, he or she will be with you for 18 years. You and your spouse will still be there, together, when your child walks out the door for college. Your relationship has to be the priority over baby making.

## Battling Midlife and Depression

**Q:** My wife is in midlife and on medication for depression. We used to have a great sex life, but now there's nothing there. She doesn't seem to have any energy. How can we get our sex life back?

**A:** Good for you for wanting your sex life back. A lot of people in midlife settle for no sex or boring sex, and that's too bad. Here are a few things you can do:

- Talk to your doctor. Some medicines lower sexual drive, but there are other options to investigate.

- To increase your spouse's energy, take a walk together in bright sunshine or sit and bask in the warm glow of the sun. Natural light does wonders to pick up the spirits of those suffering from depression.

- Spice up your sex life with some variety. Your spouse may remember what sex was like before depression, and the idea of it may be exhausting. She may think, *No way can I do that again. I don't have enough energy.* So try something different. (See the Friday chapter for ideas.)

What's most important is that you step back into the water. She may or may not be able to climax, so don't make that your goal. Keep your intimacy high in the little things you do throughout the day—a gentle kiss on the back of the neck, a stroking of the hair, a smile. For people who are depressed, knowing someone cares and finds them attractive can make a big difference on their road to recovery.

## I Miss My Wife

**Q:** My wife has been career oriented since the day we met, and I've been on the career track too. But lately she's been traveling a lot since her job responsibilities increased. I miss my wife being home. I know that sounds whiny, and I don't mean to be that way, but I don't know how else to say it. My wife's really competent, and I respect her for all she's accomplished in the workforce. But I miss seeing her in the kitchen in the morning, laughing with me over our days, and warming our bed. I'll just say it: I'm lonely. How can I tell her that without making her feel guilty? She's got a lot on her plate right now, and I don't want to add more. That wouldn't be fair.

**A:** The best way to say it is just to say it, without guilt-tripping her or giving her the puppy-dog eyes. She's a businesswoman, so be straightforward but gentle. "Honey, I'm so proud of you and all you're accomplishing. You're a major force to be reckoned with in the workplace, and you're moving mountains. I'd never want to change that, because it's part of who you are. But I have to admit that I really miss you. You are so important to me, and your presence is important to me. Texting and talking on the phone aren't the same as spending time with you. I'm feeling lonely, to be honest."

Suggest that the two of you consider ways you can spend more time together. It might include her adapting her workload so she takes fewer travel assignments. If your job is portable, you might be able to travel with her sometimes, so at least you're together at the hotel at night and in the morning. If you're home, why not tackle some of the tasks she would normally do? That will free her up for more fun and marital intimacy when she is home. Otherwise that multitasking, efficient woman will be determined to get the basic cleaning tasks done in the precious hours she is home.

In other words, you give a little, she gives a little. Marriage is a partnership.

## Sexual Interest Waning in Menopause

**Q:** My wife is starting to go through menopause, and her interest in sex is waning. Is this normal, and how or when will these feelings settle?

**A:** When a woman enters menopause, common changes that occur are drops in estrogen, skin sensitivity, and less ability to lubricate. For example, maybe she used to love it when you touched her inner thighs, but now she finds that touch irritating and complains that your hands feel like sandpaper. Or she might say that when you enter her now and start to rub, it's painful.

If you realize the changes that will occur, you can help to remedy them. She can see her doctor for products that will help with the estrogen drop. You can soften your hands with lotion (yes, even real men use it), and also experiment with a lighter stroke and vary the body areas you touch. You should also have a stock of different types of lubricants and learn to use them freely.

What's vital, though, is how both of you respond mentally to the changes. The mind is one of the most important sex organs each of you has. If you deal with the changes with a sense of humor and are okay with exploring new ways to do things, you'll do just fine.

The good news? Postmenopausal women report they have a renewed interest in sex, are more enthusiastic about it, and feel more free now that they don't have to consider the possibility of becoming pregnant.

## Everything Has to Be Perfect

**Q:** My wife has a tough time having sex unless everything is just perfect—the kids aren't home, the sheets are perfectly clean, the dog has been fed, the neighbors are on vacation . . . you see where I'm going with this. That means sex doesn't happen very often for us. Any ideas how to step over this obstacle?

**A:** I can relate. My lovely wife was always concerned about waking the children in our private time. Kids, in-laws, and neighbors can all be interruptions. So invest in a really good lock for your bedroom door and use it frequently. Swap some babysitting to provide a kid-free zone for your marital fest. Make a reservation and invite your wife out for a little fling. It doesn't have to be the Ritz-Carlton—even a Motel 6 will do. Just go anywhere and do something that is out of the regular pace of life. Sure, it may cost you a few bucks. But isn't she worth investing in? There's nothing that will pay you more dividends long term than your marriage.

# *Wednesday*

## Someone's in Bed with You . . .

And it's not only your spouse. How to identify the intruders and reclaim the space for the two of you.

### I Tend to Blow

**Q:** I know I have a problem with anger. When I get upset, I blow. Half an hour later, I'm over it. But my wife takes any blowup personally, even if I am only upset about work or the garden hose breaking. Hours later she's still miffed. How can I get her to realize that sometimes guys just get angry, but then we get over it? And if I'm over it, why can't she get over it too?

**A:** We all get angry. It's a natural emotion. But how you control your anger has everything to do with how your wife will respond to you relationally. Let me paint a scene for you. You're sick with the flu, and you say to yourself, "Oh, if only I could hurl, then I know I'd feel better." So you hurl and feel better momentarily, until you have to hurl again. Then you look around and see the huge mess you've made all over the bathroom rug.

When you blow, you're hurling your anger all over your wife, and that doesn't feel good. It's not a little thing either. Right now anger is controlling your home and short-circuiting your marital intimacy. Your wife will hold back because she's afraid of getting hurt emotionally. And who can blame her? A woman needs to feel the security and reassurance of consistent love during the day to desire sexual intimacy, which is the ultimate closeness, in the evening.

Instead of emitting fiery blasts in your wife's presence, find new ways to handle your anger. Work out for an hour at a gym before you come home. Take a walk to detox. Add a punching bag in the garage—it's fairly inexpensive and effective therapy. When anger builds, head out to the garage and go a few rounds.

There's something else you should consider too. If you struggle with a hot temper, you likely saw it patterned in your home as you were growing up. Perhaps your father lashed out in anger, and your submissive mother simply took it. You watched those interchanges between the two adults closest to you and thought, *So that's how you deal with things that go wrong. You blow.* If so, the pattern of anger is deeply ingrained in your personality as the first go-to coping tool. Yes, you can deal with it on your own, but it would help to have someone outside your family hold you accountable—someone you respect because of their years of wisdom, or a professional counselor.

Home should not be a place where anyone fears verbal abuse and bouts of anger. It must be a place of safety, security, and unconditional love. You have some work to do. But I believe in you. If you put your mind to it and gather support to hold you accountable, you'll be on the right track in no time.

## How Honest Should I Be?

**Q:** My spouse was a virgin when we got married. I wasn't, but my bride-to-be didn't know that. I always skirted the question because I had tried hard to put my promiscuous past behind me. Yet sometimes when we make love, images of faces from one-night stands pop into my head. I know the past is the past, so how honest should I be now? I couldn't tell her before we married. I was afraid I'd lose her if she knew what my previous life had been like. Hers was so different. Should I tell her now, or is it better for her not to know? And if I tell her, how much do I tell her?

**A:** A healthy marriage cannot be built on a lie or a skirting of the truth. Your spouse needs to know you were not a virgin and that you had multiple past partners. Both of you should immediately be tested for venereal diseases to make sure you haven't passed something to her.

But even more painful than the physical aspect of danger—you involving her in your chain of multiple sex partners—is the emotional fallout. She trusted you. Because you skirted the question and didn't tell her the truth, she assumed you were a virgin. That means she didn't have the opportunity to choose whether she was willing to take the risk of contracting a sexual disease. You made that choice for her.

If your spouse is furious, that's understandable. Risking your own life is one thing, but risking hers without her knowledge is something entirely different.

You can't go back and change the past, but you can choose to be honest now. Don't give details about past sexual partners; she merely needs to know that you had many and that you both should be tested. Until you're tested and cleared, don't have sex. Allow her time and space to process this news and her feelings of betrayal. Realize that you will need to work extra hard to prove that you are trustworthy, since you have broken her confidence.

The road back to marital intimacy will be difficult, but you can do it if both parties are willing.

## My Ex Still Makes Demands

**Q:** I've been divorced for four years. I remarried a year ago, but my ex still insists that he be invited to all the family parties. My husband, who's a great guy, disagrees vehemently. "He's the one who chose to leave you," he says. "So why should he get a say in the matter? I don't want him here." My ex doesn't pay any child support but declares that he has rights to see the kids. I'm torn. My ex is, after all, my kids' dad, but I don't want to go against my husband's wishes.

My husband truly loves my girls, who are six and seven, and they love him. Because he was my friend for a couple of years before we dated, the girls always remember him in their life. They don't remember much, if anything, of their dad from when they were babies. To them he's just a guy who shows up at family parties and gives them presents. They don't seem that comfortable with him either. They always run to my husband and stay by him when their dad shows up. Still, my ex is their dad. What should I do?

**A:** I think you already answered your own question. You merely need the courage to stand by your decision. If your girls see your husband more as their dad, why do you want your ex hanging around—unless he's been court-ordered to do so and is making child-support payments? Not only did he leave you in the lurch with two toddlers, but he's not helping out financially. Your girls clearly aren't comfortable with him. Your husband now *is* their daddy in their minds and hearts. The only things hanging over you are your guilt for a marriage that didn't work out and some misplaced guilt that just because your ex contributed biologically to the birth of the girls, he should have rights to the rest of their lives.

Contributing some sperm doesn't make a relationship between a dad and a daughter. Being a daily part of their lives, loving them unconditionally, and providing for them do. You said twice that your ex is the kids' dad, so clearly that's where you feel torn. But honestly, is that deadbeat guy really their dad, when the girls can't even remember him? Your husband is not only a smart, protective man, but he's right. Your ex should have no say in the matter. A little trip to court should do the trick. And if not, a restraining order is due.

**We Can't Agree**

**Q:** We thought we agreed on everything before we got married—and that we got along so well. Then we got married. Now we fight more than we make love. Most of our fights are about sex—what we should do during sex, what we shouldn't do during sex, what she wants, what I want. It's dampening our sex life . . . and making us cranky with each other in everything else. What do you do when you can't seem to agree?

**A:** It's easy to do things in the short haul, when a relationship is new and you both feel "romantic." The true test of a marriage is in the long haul. When you said "I do," you thought only two of you were saying those vows, didn't you? But more people were involved. Your parents and your spouse's parents—and stepparents, if there were any—all have an impact on who you are and who your spouse is.

Everything you and your wife learned in your homes is influencing who you're becoming as a couple. Perhaps your spouse didn't grow up in a home where sex was a comfortable subject. In fact, it was seen as something you just have to do to procreate.

Is it any wonder, then, if your spouse doesn't want to have sex until you're ready to have kids? If you grew up in a home where pleasure was important as well as spontaneity, it's no wonder the two of you are butting heads.

Both of you need a time-out together. Discuss what each of you expects out of sex. What counts as sex in your perspective? How often do you have sex? What kind of sex is okay and not okay? All of those expectations are part of the unwritten rulebook that you and your bride individually carried to your wedding. If you don't identify what those expectations are, you'll always have unhappy discussions avoiding the issues. So identify them and figure out a way to compromise so each of you feels comfortable. Then watch your sex life soar.

Most of all, kick mom and dad and mom-in-law and dad-in-law out of bed. This is *your* marriage. You make the rules . . . together.

Have fun doing it!

## Addicted to Porn

**Q:** I got the shock of my life when I discovered porn on my husband's computer recently. Worse, when I confronted him, he said he'd started looking at it years ago, when he was a teenager. His older brother had introduced him to it. I feel sick, used, and betrayed, knowing that when we had sex, he had all those perverted images in his head. Now some of the things he's wanted to try that make me uncomfortable make sense. But no way can I stack up against the hot women doing those unmentionable things on the screen. Nor do I want to.

The night I found those disgusting pictures, I walked out of the house. I couldn't stand to stay there or to sleep in our bed, where we've had sex. I love my husband, but I don't want to compete with those girls. He needs help; I need help; we need help. But where do we even start?

**A:** He's addicted to porn, just like alcoholics are addicted to alcohol. There isn't an easy fix. But there's also something you need to know. Pornography is not a relational temptation; it's a visual temptation. Men are visually stimulated by pornography. They can use the pictures to stimulate an erection. They're usually not seeking a relationship with the girl or woman; that feminine figure is only a picture on a page or screen. What the men are seeking is a physical release of sexual tension for themselves. Married men who view pornography on a regular basis are also those who seek variety in sex and often have wives who are uncomfortable with variety.

It's not unusual for a man to be introduced to pornography when he's a teenager and exploring sexuality for the first time. However, at a time when he's learning how to relate to the opposite gender, viewing pornography can skew his view of women. Those images of pornography are indelibly imprinted on his brain, subject to recall at any time. Does your husband view and treat you in a positive light? Does he express appreciation for what you do? Does he admire who you are? Or does he denigrate you, telling you you're not good enough, you never do enough, etc.?

When someone views pornography for a lengthy period, the line between the people onscreen and those in real life starts to blur. A man begins to see women as objects of lust to be used and discarded, instead of human beings you talk to and empathize with, who have their own problems, hopes, and desires. Sadly, many of the women who enter the pornography industry are taking what they think is a step to a better life—more money, the ability to get away from home and out on their own. Instead, they are trapped by a vicious industry that uses and abuses them. So when you think of pornography, view those women with sadness rather than as "the other women" in your husband's life who you have to compete with.

You feel betrayed and used, and rightfully so. Life can't go on for either of you in its current state. You need to confront your husband in a truthful but loving way. Let him know you feel hurt and violated in your marriage after discovering the pictures. Tell him eyeball to eyeball if at all possible, since it will be more difficult for him to avoid the look of betrayal in your eyes. If you can't do that in an emotionally even manner (yelling in anger will only cut off both your conversation now and any attempt in the future), write him a letter. Hand it to him, put it in his briefcase, or mark it "personal" and stash it on the dash of his car.

Let's say tonight, when both of you are in bed together, he all of a sudden touches you with his toe. You know exactly what that means. It's his little way of saying, "Hey, I'm here, and I'm interested." When you get that signal, turn and look him in the eye. Say bluntly, "The farthest thing from my mind right now is having sex with you. I am very hurt. I feel our marriage has been cheapened." Don't pull any punches on the language. He needs straightforward talk, because he needs to feel the full impact of his choices and realize how they are affecting your marriage. If he doesn't, he'll continue to stay involved in pornography. He'll warp your sex life, continue to hurt you, and ultimately completely ruin your marriage.

Because your husband has been looking at porn long term and is addicted, he needs to get some counseling from a trusted professional. Should you go with him? No. He needs to face the music himself. You didn't get him into this situation. He got himself into it. Even though it was his older brother who introduced him to porn, he still had the choice whether to look . . . and whether to keep looking. Every person has a choice about what they will view and not view.

Pornography is a huge, multibillion-dollar business in the United States alone. You have to take a tough stand on this issue. Your husband needs help, and he needs it now. While he's going through counseling for his issues, you might benefit from some similar help in dealing with your own feelings. Tackling the issue of pornography and the relational fallout isn't something you can handle on your own.

### Gave In Too Soon

**Q:** We dated for three years before we got married. Both of us made a vow early on that we didn't want sex to enter our relationship until we were married. We held to our promise until a week before our wedding. Then, at the height of wedding stress, one thing led to another when we were alone, and we ended up going all the way. After that, our honeymoon was a disappointment. When we had sex on our wedding night, I found it hard to get an erection. My bride said, "That's okay, I'd rather go to sleep anyway." Wow. Now we can have all the sex we want, but we don't want it anymore. What's wrong with us?

**A:** Let's say you've studied hard for a test. But right before you take it, you cheat by buying someone's notes. Understandably you're going to feel some guilt about the results, no matter what they are. You'll always wonder what your score would have been if you hadn't cheated.

What you did is a lot like cheating on a test. When both of you hold to a commitment for three years not to have sex but then break it a week before the grand event, what is that saying to each other about the way you keep promises?

The guilt you feel from breaking that promise is now wreaking havoc on your sex life. That guilt is the elephant in your bedroom, and until you address what's sitting right on your bed with you, it won't go away.

Have a frank discussion with your bride. "I feel really guilty about having sex with you before we got married. I wanted that first time to be really special . . . and it was . . . but I'd wanted it to be after I said 'I do' and made that promise to you."

I know saying "I'm sorry" is antiquated in today's culture, but forgiveness goes a long way in relationships. Ask your bride, "Will you forgive me for breaking my promise that I wouldn't have sex with you before we got married?"

Chances are, she's feeling the same way, or she may simply be feeling emotional distance from you but she's not sure why. The two of you need to agree you broke your promise, talk about how you feel about that, and then vow faithfulness and loyalty to each other all over again. If you do that, what happens next in your bedroom can be better than you could ever imagine . . . minus the guilt that's holding you back.

## My Spouse Had an Affair

**Q:** My spouse had an affair. She says she didn't mean for it to happen, but it did. It was a one-night thing, and she vows it will never happen again. I believe her, but still, it happened. I love my wife and want to stay married to her, but I'm also shocked and hurt she would do something like that. Where do we go from here?

**A:** When there is an affair in a marriage, there are only two directions you can go.

*Option 1: Move onward to forge a stronger relationship and to safeguard your marriage.* To get there, you have to talk about the affair—only with each other, no friends—and get to the root of why it happened. As you sort things out, this information needs to stay between the two of you. You don't need others' input to make your road of reconciliation more difficult. Critical questions need to be asked: Why was your wife drawn to the arms of another man? What is lacking in your relationship? It is not your fault that your wife fell into another man's arms—that was her choice—but why was she feeling lonely and vulnerable enough to do so? Is warmth and intimacy missing in your relationship? If you don't have a love affair with your spouse, someone else will.

So, as you move on, discuss together: What can you do differently? What can she do differently? Does your wife feel bonded to you? Do you open your heart to her? Or are the two of you disconnected, living your own lives? If so, it's no surprise that she was searching for someone she could connect and bond to. Women crave relationship. Without it they feel empty and alone.

Also, you will need to grapple with your thoughts and feelings of betrayal. You can forgive, but you can't forget. In fact, you shouldn't forget. You should forgive and remember, so you can take steps to protect your marriage.

It would be wise for your wife to step away from the situation that introduced the affair—whether it was a job, an organization where she volunteers, etc.—so she is not in a close working relationship with or in close proximity to that man. If she can't walk away from the situation, you need to be physically present with her wherever possible. She needs to admit that what she did was wrong, tell you, "I'm so sorry for what I did and the pain I caused you," and ask you for forgiveness.

If you want your marriage to not only survive but have the possibility of flourishing, you need to extend that forgiveness and then avoid digging up the bone in the yard down the road. You both should spend time figuring out what went wrong and what you can do differently in the future, then express your love and commitment to each other.

Answer the following questions together:

217

- Before you found out about (or had) the affair, how would you rate your marital relationship on a scale of 1 (terrible) to 10 (best)? Why did you give it this rating?
- Where would you like your relationship to be?
- What would it take to move your relationship from where it is now to where you'd like it to be? What kinds of steps can you take together each day?

When you ask these three questions, answer them honestly, and brainstorm how to get from point A to point B, you participate in the formation of a healthy, growing relationship that can stand the test of any future temptations of affairs.

You as the husband will also need to discipline your mind not to go to thoughts of your wife with that other man. And your wife needs to discipline her mind not to think of him. Both of you must focus on establishing each other as the number-one priority.

Going this direction entails a lot of humility, vulnerability, discipline, and letting go of any bitterness to work together toward the end result: building up your relationship to protect it from affairs in the future. That means spending a significant amount of time together to strengthen your marriage. When your wife goes out of town on business to where she met that colleague or attends the PTA meeting where she met that stay-at-home dad, you go with her.

Develop shared hobbies. Put each other first and say no to a lot of social engagements that draw you away from each other or put you in a roomful of people where you barely see each other. Basically, "redate" each other.

Your wife will need to prove she is trustworthy. For example, you may feel the need to call and check in with her when she's apart from you. She has to accept that as a result of her infidelity. Both of you should call each other often and check in to keep your hearts more closely connected.

Never ever talk to your friends or relatives about the affair. You don't want the "feedback" or gossip of others to make your road harder. If your relationship is stalling out, go to a trusted

---

### If You Had an Affair

If you are the one who had the affair, follow these steps now to safeguard your marriage in the future:

- Get what happened out in the open. No secrets between you and your spouse. You need to answer any and all questions about who the affair was with, how it started, how long it continued, and if or how it concluded. But be careful about sharing specific details that happened between you sexually; that is often more information than your spouse should have or is able to bear.
- End all contact with the person you had the affair with—no phone calls, no letters, no emails, not even "casual" meetings. Cut off all ties. That may mean, if the person is a co-worker, you quit that job and find another. But isn't your marriage more important than any job? Get rid of all items—clothing or gifts—that person has given you. Give away the clothes you were wearing when you had the affair. Better yet, burn them as a symbol that what was in the past will not happen again.
- If you have had sex with your spouse since the affair, both of you need to be checked out medically for potential venereal diseases. If you haven't had sex since the affair, you alone need to be tested, receive the results, and share them with your spouse before you have sex again. You have no idea who your sexual partner hooked up with before he hooked up with you.
- If your sexual partner purposely runs into you, tell him the affair is over and you don't want to be in contact with him. If he texts you, don't respond. Immediately report the meeting or the text to your spouse. Allow him to decide what to do with that text; some spouses will respond, telling that sexual partner to back off, and others will simply delete the message. Changing phone numbers would be a good idea. Your revitalized relationship needs to be based on no lies, no deception. Only honesty will help you move forward.

---

professional for counseling. Say your marriage vows to each other again, and start over.

Can you make it? Yes, you can. Is it messy? Yes. But how you respond to this situation and the patience you have in resolving it will make or break your marriage. Working through betrayal and anger will take time, communication, an agreement to resolve conflicts that come up swiftly and sensitively, and a process of forgiveness.

For most couples who live through an affair, it takes about 18 to 24 months to rebuild the trust in their relationship. It's like fabric that has been ripped. It might look all right lying there in a heap, but as soon as you lift it up to the light, you see the holes and the damage that moths have done. Affairs are like that—some of the resulting holes can take a while to show up. One of the biggest rips is in trust. When you're apart, it's important to call or text frequently to keep in touch and share what's happening in your day and in your heart.

The work is worth it. You really don't want to step toward option 2.

*Option 2: March toward divorce court and don't look back.* Sounds easy, doesn't it? Nothing to work through relationally. Just let the attorneys do the talking.

But what looks like a quick fix to a hurting relationship isn't as easy as it seems—for you, your spouse, or any children you might have. It's agony to tear apart two people who have become one through marriage. It's a lifelong trauma neither will forget. And if you have children, they'll be stuck in the middle of a court process. Every child deserves to go to sleep with sugarplums dancing in her head, not the sight of her parents battling it out in court over her.

Let me be blunt. If you can't work together with your spouse— the person you chose to marry—through this road bump and fix this relationship, what makes you think you can enter a new relationship someday and manage the road bumps with that person?

For your own sake, your spouse's sake, and your children's sake, consider option 1 first. Especially since this was a onetime affair. A pattern of affairs is something far different—it's tough to have any relationship with a person who isn't committed to you.

## He Isn't Interested in Sex

**Q:** My husband pursued me passionately when we were dating. We talked late into the night every night, he brought me flowers, and he wooed me. I guess I thought it would always be like that when we got married. And I couldn't wait for the sex. But once we got married, he seemed disinterested in sex. And all the wonderful heart-to-hearts we had faded away. I shouldn't complain—he's always kind and helpful and will do anything I ask. Yet I can't help but feel a little disappointed. Is this really all marriage is? I want to be wooed again, and I long to be close to him. Yet now he keeps his distance.

**A:** There are multiple possibilities for what's going on in your relationship.

First, I'd suggest that the two of you go to your doctor and have some tests done. Are there physiological reasons for why your husband is disinterested in sex? Was he always that way? Or has his loss of interest in sex been a gradual progression?

Second, if the doctor visit doesn't reveal some solutions, I suggest you visit a counselor. It is possible that your husband may have grown up in a Victorian-style home where sex was seen as something you don't talk about and you don't do. An event in his childhood may have triggered his thinking that sex is something dirty or nasty. He may have been sexually abused by a man or a woman. If so, there are some issues you will need to work through in order to have the intimate connection both of you deserve in marriage.

There is also a third possible reason. If a man seems to be a ready teddy for sex but then, once you're married, that interest wanes quickly and he becomes disinterested in you and disconnected, it's highly possible that he's a homosexual or has homosexual leanings. Many gay men and women hide out in marriage, thinking that being married will change their orientation and feelings—especially if they've grown up with conservative values. The guilt they feel drives them to try to do what their background tells them is "normal"—marry a person of the opposite sex and establish a family.

So yes, you can just let things ride and be happy for the helpful man you've got. But your question tells me you are longing for something more.

The way to start going after that something more is by kicking off a discussion with the man you love. Start with the medical doctor first. Then proceed to the counselor. If the third option is a possibility, the counselor will help you and your husband discover that in a safe setting.

## How to Win Her Back?

**Q:** Last week was our third anniversary, and instead of the sex fest I had in mind for the evening, my wife celebrated it by telling me when I got home that she was done being a servant. She'd packed her bags and was going to stay with a friend for a while. "If you really love me," she said, "you'll think about the way you've been treating me." I must have looked confused, because right before she walked out the door, she added, "Maybe you'll discover that anything having to do with the house isn't my job; it's our job. But since you can't help, I guess you'll need to do it all on your own to get the picture."

I was stunned. My wife works part-time, and I always thought that taking care of the cooking, laundry, cleaning, etc., was the

other part of her job. It didn't enter my brain that I should be helping with it since I work full-time and she's home half of each day.

Dr. Leman, I really love my wife. She means everything to me.
I want her back and I want to change, but I have no idea how to
start winning her back.

**A:** Let me ask you a question. Are you a firstborn or only child?
Did you grow up in a house with a critical-eyed parent, where
your dad's method was the right and only way, and you better
hop to it? Did he believe that a woman's place was in the home,
that your mother should be subservient to her husband in all
things, and that her desires were not important? And when you
grew up, did you say you'd never be like him, but you're exactly
like him in your own marriage?

Have you been a controller, demanding your wife do specific
things for you at specific times—such as have dinner prepared
by 6:00 p.m. each day? What have you done to help her? Instead
of doing the dishes because she cooked dinner, do you head for
that comfortable couch to get in some TV time?

House stuff isn't only for women; it's not "their job" just because they're women. There are two of you living in that house,
and you both should pull your weight. My guess is that you also
grew up with a pleaser mom, who bent over backwards to smooth
your pathway in life and did whatever your dad wanted when he
wanted it. So you assumed your wife would do the same things
and act the same way as your mom. Frankly, good for your wife
that she has a backbone. Sounds like you've been running over
her, even though you didn't realize it.

However, now that you know, it's time to step up to the plate
and be the kind of helpmate to your wife that she deserves. If
you want to win her back, clean the house, learn how to cook
a meal, and then tell her you love her and invite her over for
dinner. Then *you* do the dishes as she talks to you. That will go
a long way toward showing her you're willing to make changes

and that she is important to you. Before you can be a Casanova in the bedroom, you have to win your wife's love and admiration by helping her out in all the other rooms of the house. It's not her work; it's your work together.

And while you're at it, get that leaky faucet fixed and change the toilet paper rolls. It's the little things that count with women and show them you mean what you say.

## Makeup Sex?

**Q:** My husband is a firstborn, the kind of guy who has to win. Whenever we fight with words, he always wins. That's because I give up. I know I can never win, so why try? But after he wins, he wants sex—to "make up." I really hate it when he says that. To him, having sex means the fight's suddenly over, like it never happened. To me, it feels like he wins twice—both the fight and the sex he wants. My body is there, but my heart is elsewhere. It's hurting, and I feel empty. If I don't agree to have sex, though, he just keeps pushing until I give in. What should I do? I'm starting to resent my husband.

**A:** Your husband is treating you like a doormat, and it needs to stop. You were not put on this earth to be used when he wants. There are two of you in this relationship, and you are equal. But he's the one doing the driving in this situation, and you're the passenger trying to get out of the car.

Chances are that he grew up in a home where his dad was an authoritarian who had the final word, running the house with an iron fist in all matters. Everybody, including his wife, did what he wanted. As a result, your husband grew up thinking that men rule and women jump to attention.

He needs a wakeup call, and the faster, the better. If you can't get on the same page with this, then the very foundation of your marriage will have a big crack that will end in both sides of your house caving in.

Both of you are created equal; you are not lesser because you are a woman. Many men from conservative backgrounds use Ephesians 5:22–24 in the Bible as clout to rule the home: "Wives, submit yourselves to your own husbands as you do to the Lord. For the husband is the head of the wife as Christ is the head of the church, his body, of which he is the Savior. Now as the church submits to Christ, so also wives should submit to their husbands in everything." They stop right there instead of reading on. But the passage adds a critical concept in the following verses: "Husbands, love your wives, just as Christ loved the church and gave himself up for her" (v. 25). Exactly how should a husband love his wife? The answer is clear: "Husbands ought to love their wives as their own bodies. . . . Each one of you also must love his wife as he loves himself, and the wife must respect her husband" (vv. 28, 33). In other words, marriage as God intended it is a mutually submissive act. A woman submits to her husband by thinking of him first. A husband submits to his wife by thinking of her first. And together they are submissive to their Creator.

## An Emotional Affair?

**Q:** My wife's job takes her out of town for a couple weeks every month or two. I really miss her during those times. The last time she was gone I had dinner with a female co-worker . . . and dinner again the next night. I don't know how it happened, but we touched and then kissed a little. We didn't go all the way, but I find myself thinking about those two nights. I've been trying to bury the memories, but I can't. I feel so guilty. Each time my wife and I have sex now, I find myself holding back. Sex is no longer satisfying because I don't feel as connected to her. Should I tell her what happened? And if so, what exactly do I tell her?

**A:** Yes, you tell her. You have to tell her . . . sensitively. If your loneliness drives you into another woman's arms when your wife is out of town, something has to change in your relationship. Although you didn't have sex, you did draw close to your co-worker emotionally. Take some time to figure out why that happened. What steps led you to consider having dinner with her? Your loneliness? The lack of a plan for your evening? Your co-worker flattering you?

False emotional intimacy can take two people farther than they want to go and keep them longer than they want to stay. So that you don't fall into the trap of an affair—emotional intimacy with someone other than your wife can lead to a physical affair—you need to fix what is missing in your relationship with your wife as swiftly as possible.

Be honest. Tell your wife how lonely you are—that you need to connect more closely and more often with her. Share that you had dinner twice with a co-worker and were drawn to her because you were so lonely. Yes, your wife will be shocked and, most likely, angry. But this situation should be a wake-up call for you as a couple. You cannot have physical closeness—satisfying sex—until you focus on developing emotional closeness as a couple. That means spending time together and meeting each other's needs.

A good relationship is a terrible thing to waste. Don't waste yours. Use this event to refocus your lives on each other. Keep your time apart to a minimum. Now would be a perfect time for you two to take that dream vacation you've always wanted . . . on a warm, sunny beach somewhere.

Have one of those little fruity drinks with the umbrella toothpick for me, would you?

## Is He a Sex Addict?

**Q:** My husband likes R-rated movies that have a lot of sex in them—too much for me. Whenever we watch them, though, we have great sex afterward. Now he wants to rent a porno flick to get us in the mood. I'm squeamish about watching other couples have sex. I think sex should be something that happens between a husband and wife, not that other people voyeuristically watch. The idea of having pornography in my home makes me feel a little sick, to be honest. I want to keep my husband happy, and I usually go along with what he wants when he wants it, but this time I'm not comfortable. How should I handle it? Could my husband be a sex addict?

**A:** When a guy is "living in the zone"—in other words, he's focused continually on sexual activity—there are recognizable symptoms. Your marriage will be affected because he's preoccupied. Yes, he may be sitting next to you in the room, but his mind isn't really there. He's addicted to sex—seeing it and experiencing it. However, in order to have sex with you, he has to "get in the mood" by seeing sex acted out by someone else first. That means there is actually a decreased interest in the sexual aspect of your marriage. Without seeing sex on the screen, he can't get an erection.

Continuing to view sex on the screen will lead to a lack of intimacy, warmth, and sensitivity within your marriage. I'll put it bluntly. Your husband is stepping onto dangerous ground, toward relational isolation, where only the portrayal of sex and experiencing it will become his focus. When that occurs, it's likely he will shut you out.

Now is the time to make an appointment with a trusted professional. No, your husband won't like it, and he may refuse to go. If he does, he's deeper into sexual addiction than you might think. In that case, go by yourself so you can understand how sexual addiction develops and what you might be able to do to help your husband.

## No Passionate Romance Here

**Q:** Our honeymoon was supposed to be the best time of our lives, or so I thought. I'd spent hours shopping for the right outfits so I could look sexy for the man I love. But our first night, he just wanted to hold hands and walk on the beach. At first I thought, *Isn't that sweet? This is so special. He's taking his time.*

Two nights later, when we still hadn't made love, I started to wonder what was going on. He didn't want to be naked with me, but when I finally pushed, he got undressed. Yet he couldn't get an erection. When I finally asked him what was wrong, he told me he had spent a lot of years struggling with homosexuality. He said he was working his way out of it, but that he needed me to be patient.

I had no idea. With his words, my hopes for a passionate romance went out the window. Now I only feel hurt and confused. But I still love him, we're such good friends, and I want to see if we can make this work. Any suggestions?

**A:** This will be hard to hear, but I need to say it plainly. If a man isn't interested in sex, he's definitely struggling with his masculinity and may have homosexual leanings. There is no male on the planet who can see his wife naked and not start thinking about rolling in the sack with her—unless he is attracted to the same sex. It's rare that such an orientation would change. Whether he acts on that, of course, is up to him.

So yes, you two can have a marriage. You can be best friends. But if he is struggling with homosexuality, there will be an element of two becoming one that you won't experience—sexual fulfillment. Only you and your husband can decide if you can live with that.

## Great Sex . . . before Marriage

**Q:** We had great sex before we got married. But now that we're married, our sex life stinks. In fact, I can count on one hand the amount of times we've had sex in the last six months. Did premarital sex ruin our sex life now?

**A:** Many couples who are physically intimate before they get married ask the same question. Somehow the thrill wears off when they tie the knot. Before marriage, sex had a secretive aspect that it doesn't have now. Also, when you were dating, you were putting your best foot forward. You always brushed your teeth or used breath mints before you kissed. Now your dragon breath in the morning isn't especially attractive. Things back then were new and exciting, and your sex life was a priority. Your sexual experiences were thrilling, like a ride on a roller coaster.

But love isn't just the feeling of a moment; it's a plan of action for a lifetime. It's a choice to put the one you love first. If sex has lost its zip, you two need to prioritize your sex life again. What does your spouse enjoy most? How will you meet that desire? When was the last time you surprised your spouse, took him or her somewhere special, and made all the arrangements yourself?

Sex isn't about finding the G-spot or the I-spot or the X-spot. It's about a relationship. If your sex life is suffering, chances are that you have unsettled issues between you. If you had sex outside of marriage with each other or anyone else, a big issue could be trust. You might wonder, *Will my spouse play around on me now that we're married?* The chances of an affair will be greatly heightened if the two of you don't talk about your disappointment and why your sex life stinks.

Is it that the thrill is gone now that you're married? If so, spice things up with some variety to get the thrill back into your relationship. If it's a lack of trust, resentment, or a lack of forgiveness for some action in the past, you need to take care of that too. Don't let the sun go down before you talk.

Some of you reading this are thinking, *Doesn't everybody have sex before they get married these days—whether with the partner they're now married to or with other people? I mean, Dr. Leman, are you from the Mesozoic era? Did you have a pet dinosaur when you were a kid?*

Nope, I'm from the real-life twenty-first century. But you're right. Few people today bat an eye about having sex before marriage. In fact, I talk with couples nationwide in all sorts of settings about that, among many other issues.

But just because a lot of people have sex before marriage doesn't mean they won't run into issues as a result later—especially those of trust. Previous sexual experience doesn't necessarily mean that you'll soar to new heights within marriage now that you can have sex anytime you feel like it. In fact, that little voice inside that prompts us to run from things that might hurt us goes into overdrive, reminding us of what we could have had—minus the guilt—if we had chosen to wait until marriage.

Look at it this way. What does the average 13-year-old girl start dreaming of? Her wedding. She imagines the man who will fall in love with her and ask her to marry him. She sees herself walking down the aisle as a vision in white.

She doesn't think, *Okay, I'll meet this guy and have sex in the back of his car when I'm 15. He'll dump me afterward because he now has the notch in his belt he wanted to boast about to other guys in the locker room. When I'm 20, I'll find the guy I'm going to marry, and we'll have better sex because I experimented when I was 15. We'll have lots of sex before we marry, just to try it out and make sure we're compatible. Then, three years later, when we have a baby on the way—much to our surprise because birth control pills are 97 percent effective—we'll finally decide to get married.*

No, the fairy tale in her head is usually quite different from the reality that often occurs. I mention this not to cause you guilt—because you can't turn back time and make different choices—but because "what might have been" may be causing you distress in your relationship now.

That little voice and the potential for STDs are why I advise couples to steer clear of premarital sex. God's original design was that sex should be reserved for marriage, and I believe wholeheartedly that's still the best plan.

There is, however, no do-over in life. Once you've had sex for the first time, you've had sex. But you can choose to give your marriage a good foundation for success by fine-tuning your marital intimacy overall. Part of that includes brainstorming ways to make sex enticing and satisfying for both of you.

With just a little work, you can create your very own thrill ride—a roller coaster of pleasure—in your bedroom. Even better, you can take as long as you want. Now that you're married, you don't have to worry about anyone walking in on you doing the mattress mambo . . . except for your little ankle-biter battalion. In that case, it might be time for you to invest in a really good lock for your bedroom door and maybe even a little soundproofing.

I highly recommend it.

# *Thursday*

## *Making Love with Words*

Why the words you choose, and how you fulfill them, determine your marital intimacy and shape your sex life.

### He Doesn't Talk

**Q:** My husband and I both work outside the home. We're DINKs (double income, no kids) and in our late twenties. When I get home, I love telling my husband about my day, but he never says much other than, "Oh, it was okay." How are we supposed to keep up with each other if he won't talk?

**A:** Both men and women long for a connection, but the type of connection they crave is different.

You want to talk to connect, and you've still got a lot of words left to use. That's because women are relationally oriented and use three and a half times the amount of words that men use on a daily basis. Your husband? By the time you both get home, he's weary and he's used up his word count. He doesn't want to blather through all the ins and outs of his day. He just wants to relax. That's why the remote control calls to him more than processing with you. Men in general don't like questions. They hate the "why" word even more. So avoid asking him questions. Instead, when something does come out of his mouth, use statements to follow up, such as, "Oh, I'd love to hear more about that."

So what can the two of you do? Each of you needs to reserve some energy for your spouse. In 30 years when you retire, will you really be saying, "Boy, I wish I would have spent more time at the office"? I doubt it. You'll be shaking your head and saying, "If only we'd taken that trip together while we still could. . . ."

Here are some suggestions from couples I know about how to handle after-work time:

- I have an intense job. I need some process time before I go home to my wife and kids, so I take 20 minutes to pick up some coffee and go sit in a nearby park. Then when I go home, I'm ready and all ears for what my wife and kids want to tell me.

- When my husband gets home from work, I'm dying to pass the kids off to him and take a break. But instead, I give him a big hug and a "Welcome home," and send him off to change clothes and take a shower. He has a half hour to regroup before he's "on." Then we talk as we eat dinner.

- We both arrive home at the same time. We set our laptops in the main hallway, meet in the kitchen, have a snack since we're both starving, and swap stories about our days for 15 minutes.

- On my commute home, I put on soothing music and start thinking about my husband—what he's told me he had to do today. That helps me refocus from what I've done all day to the challenges he might have faced. Then I'm more sensitive to his feelings and moods. Sometimes he wants to talk. Other times he doesn't.

- We make dinner our connection time with the kids. But we do the dishes and cleanup as a couple, and no kids are allowed in the kitchen. It's our time to talk with no inter- ruptions. Then we don't have to cram that in at bedtime and can focus on other things that are far more fun. And because we've already shared our hearts and the day's happenings with each other, neither of us has to guess if the other will want sex. Either we just snuggle or we know we can go for it. It's amazing what a little communication over dishes can do.

Take it from a guy who has dishpan hands. I've done a lot of dishes in my lifetime. I'm on social security, and I still enjoy sex with my bride multiple times a week. Communication is a two-way street that reaps phenomenal rewards in your marital intimacy.


## Two Very Different Backgrounds

**Q:** I come from an Italian family. We're very big on expressing ourselves. We weep loudly, cry loudly, and converse loudly when the pasta is slightly overdone. When we were dating, my girl- friend always said she loved being a part of my family, because everybody hugged her and greeted her when she walked in the door. She's an only child, and her house was always quiet since both her parents worked.

Now that we're married, though, she wants to visit my fam- ily less and less. It didn't help that she made a dish to bring to a family dinner once, and my sister said she should add more oregano and olive oil, because it wasn't spicy enough and was too dry. I love my family, and being part of them is important to me. But my wife gets very quiet around them and then retreats as soon as she gets home. After an incredible meal at my folks', I'm ready for a rendezvous with my wife, if you know what I mean. But she is definitely not in the mood. How can we cross this chasm?

**A:** Let's make this simple. Your wife came from a quiet home; yours is loud and boisterous. How do you feel when you visit her home? Uncomfortable? Well, your wife feels the same way. Hugs can be wonderful . . . until someone criticizes her cooking, especially if she's gone the second mile to impress your family.

Only children don't like criticism very well to begin with—they've already had it dished out in boatloads by both their parents, since they're the only child to focus parental attention on. Only children are also perfectionists. If they can't do things perfectly, they feel like they have failed. So let me translate for you. When your sister told your wife to add more oregano and olive oil, your wife felt like a failure. Her cooking wasn't good enough, which meant she wasn't good enough—for you or for your family. In fact, every time she visits your family's house, that failure is drilled more deeply into her psyche and heart.

Would you want to go somewhere if you always felt like a failure there? Ah, now you're getting the picture.

Here are a few suggestions for the future:

- When you go to your family's home, don't ask your wife to bring a dish to contribute. Her cooking will never be the same as or match your mama's cooking, so she'll always feel like she's failing, even if her dish is delicious.
- Limit the amount of time you're at your parents'. Do you really have to kill a whole afternoon and evening, or would an hour over dinner be enough time to reconnect with your family, exchange some conversation, and splurge on great Italian food?

- Give your wife a break sometimes. Let her stay home and soak in the tub. You go to your parents' house for an hour and return with some delectable leftovers for her. Light a candle, tell her how special she is, and say why you had to hurry home to her.

If you try these things, you'll be surprised at the inner fires you might stir. I assure you, they'll be way better than eating your mama's cannoli.

## What's the Right Amount of Sex?

**Q:** The two of us can never agree on how much sex is the right amount. I want "too much sex," she says. I say, "But you don't want enough." Which of us is right?

**A:** You've got one thing going for you—at least the two of you are communicating about it. Now we need to get you both on the same page.

One of the biggest things couples fight over in sex is frequency—how often should you be intimate? The answer is that it will change from time to time, and you have to go with the flow. When you're under stress, you will be less likely to want to go all the way into intercourse. That doesn't mean you shouldn't eagerly enter into it if your spouse is ready for it. Usually the guy is the aggressor and wants sex more than the woman, but that can be flip-flopped. So maybe you need to dial back a bit in pursuing sex and dial up your intimacy quotient (the cuddling, the caressing, doing little things to show her how precious she is to you) if you want more pleasure in the bedroom.

Here's what I mean. I travel quite a bit for my job. But when I'm home or when my wife and I are traveling together, I bring her a cup of coffee in the morning. I also scratch her back on top of her nightie, in an S-shape, just the way she likes it. Do I do those things only because I want sex? No, I do them because my wife is the most valuable person on this earth to me, and I want her to be happy. Because I put her first, it is then much easier for her to seek my best and to meet my needs—which, even for a guy my age, means sex.

## We Dated Online

**Q:** My husband and I met online through a dating service. Since we lived several states apart, our relationship progressed mostly through emailing, texting, and phoning. We didn't even meet in person until we'd dated for four months. That weekend, we fell madly in love and got spontaneously engaged. We just knew we were perfect for each other. Two months later we married. We've now been married for three months. We used to be able to talk about everything. But now we have trouble talking at all and end up fighting. What happened to all the intimacy we thought we had?

**A:** It's not so much about what's happened in the past three months as it is about what happened before you got married. Since you were physically distanced from each other for the majority of your dating, you developed great verbal skills to compensate for that in getting to know each other. But meeting for a weekend isn't the same as dating face-to-face in the same town for at least a two-year period. That amount of time gives you the opportunity to see each other at your best and at your worst. When you see each other only once in a while, there are a lot of personality traits that can remain hidden. So it's important for those who meet online not only to text, email, and talk by phone but to spend a significant amount of time together in person as their interest in each other grows.

Without that face-to-face time, you can sometimes think you're falling in love, but you've actually fallen in need. After all, there was a reason you were on that online dating service—because you really wanted a relationship, you really wanted to be married. Then you "met" someone who approved of you, affirmed you, and said sweet things to you. For a woman especially, the exchange of information and dialogue is critical and can make some couples think they're closer than they actually are.

In short, the foundation that you laid for your relationship may not be as firm as you thought. That's why you're fighting. Now that you've chosen to marry, you owe it to yourselves to really get to know each other. That means you need to date each other. Start over in talking about the things that matter. Yes, the two of you may have exchanged information and stories online, but that's not the same as you seeing the flicker of pain in his eyes when he talks about his difficult relationship with his dad. It's not the same as him realizing how uncomfortable you feel wearing a bathing suit in front of anyone.

Here are a few tips for getting to know each other:

- Make couple time a priority whenever you're not working. Other friends, relatives, and events can wait. Your relationship has to come first.
- Tune in to each other's thoughts and feelings all throughout the day. Touch each other when you share stories. That cements your marital bond even more physiologically.
- Talk eye to eye. One of the best places I've found to do this is in the bathtub, facing each other. If you're built like me—a bullfrog on the side of a pond—or you've got a few bucks in your pocket, invest in a Jacuzzi. The point is, find a place where you can talk eyeball to eyeball without interference. It's hard to get upset with another person on any issue if they're facing you naked.

239

As you begin to talk intimately in person, you'll get to know each other in a deeper way than you thought possible, and your satisfaction in every aspect of your relationship will increase. As respect grows, you'll fight less and talk more. This "dream person" you discovered and dated online really will become the spouse of your dreams.

## Tell the Truth . . . but in Love

**Q:** I believe in telling things like they are, and so does my wife. We both grew up in homes where issues weren't sugarcoated. Our parents just said what needed to be said. Sure, our feelings got hurt sometimes, but they believed honesty was always the best policy. My wife and I agreed when we got married that we wanted the same type of relationship—where we always tell the truth to each other and don't cover things up. Still, every time I share with her things that she should have done differently or areas in which she needs to improve, she gets miffed. Then the temperature in our bedroom turns arctic and stays that way for a long time. But when she tells me what she wants me to do differently, I'm supposed to take it. What gives?

**A:** Wow, both of you are competing with each other for who can be the most blunt, aren't you? Ouch. I'm surprised your bedroom hasn't permanently frozen over into the arctic region. Being critical will never get either of you anywhere. There's a difference between telling the truth like it is—bluntly and straightforwardly—and telling the truth kindly, gently, and with love as your intent.

Yes, you should be honest with each other and not cover things up, but I can hear the attitude coming through loud and clear in your question. If you've got a critical eye and you turn that on your wife outside the bedroom, then how do you expect her to be all warm toward you inside the bedroom? And ditto for your wife.

Both of you need a charm and kindness course, or you're going to find yourselves somewhere you don't want to be—divorce court.

Since you're the one asking the question, you need to be the one who backs off first. The next time she tells you something she thinks you need to hear, say calmly, "I'll think of ways I can change that about myself. I appreciate you sharing that with me." Stay steady, and don't combat her "truth" with truths about her. One of you needs to start thawing the tundra and to keep thawing it. Fighting with words is an act of cooperation—it takes two. If you withdraw from the fight, you'll be amazed at how much kinder each of your words will become toward each other. And that will go a long way toward turning your bedroom into a little igloo with a fire stoked and burning inside.

### *Sex* Is a Taboo Word

**Q:** We do it, so how come we can't talk about it? It seems like *sex* is a taboo word in our house. Anytime I try to make any suggestions about things we could do differently, my spouse says, "Uh, let's not talk about that." Doesn't that seem a little crazy to you?

**A:** Yes, it's crazy—but common. Many men and women are embarrassed to talk about sex. From my research, I've found that couples spend 1 percent of their sexual time together talking about sex and 99 percent of that time making love. Most of the reticence stems from their upbringing—sex was pictured as something hidden, dirty, or secretive.

But sex, done God's way, should include talking about it. Check out the sexiest book in the Bible—the Song of Solomon (also known as the Song of Songs). Those two lovers talked to each other—they described each other in some of the most sensuous language you'll find anywhere. Modesty is good, but modesty in the bedroom between husband and wife is not.

Read Proverbs 5 too. It's not only great poetry but also graphically sensual about lovers:

> May you rejoice in [your] wife. . . .
> A loving doe, a graceful deer—
>   may her breasts satisfy you always,
>   may you ever be intoxicated with her love.
>
> verses 18–19

If either or both of you grew up in a home where talking about sex was taboo, then the two of you need to lie in bed together, unclothed, and read a few lines at a time of the entire book of Song of Solomon and Proverbs 5. Let your fingers do the walking as different body parts are mentioned, and see what happens. I guarantee you won't get past the first chapter of the Song of Solomon without some rapturous passion.

## The Three Most Powerful Words: "I Am Sorry"

**Q:** My wife recently attended her 10-year high school reunion weekend with a girlfriend. When I picked her up from the airport and asked her how it went, she just said, "Oh, fine, but I'm kinda tired." I took her at her word and didn't press for more details.

A few days later, I saw that she'd posted a photo of her, her friend, and three more classmates on Facebook. A guy I didn't know had his arm around her, a little too close for my comfort, so I asked her about it. She said they'd dated in high school for a couple of years before they went off to college.

It was the first I'd heard of it, and that ticked me off. "Yeah, well, he probably kissed you . . . a lot," I told her. I admit I was fishing for details.

"He did." She glared at me. "And he's a good kisser too." She went out the front door in a huff.

As soon as she walked out, I realized how stupid I'd been. I love my wife. She means everything to me. What's wrong with me that I said that to her?

She's been at her mother's house now for two days and won't talk to me when I call. What can I do to make it right? To make her come home? I really miss her.

**A:** First, you can't *make* your wife do anything. What she does is her choice. But there are some things you can do. Start with admitting to yourself you were a jealous idiot and that you handled the situation poorly. Then get on your white steed (your car) and hightail it to your mom-in-law's with your wife's favorite flowers in hand. Assume the penitent position—on your knees—and admit that same thing to her. You're a smart guy—you captured her hand in marriage, didn't you? So don't be stupid now. Two days have already gone by. Don't miss any more time with the woman you love.

Sure, your wife dated that other guy, but she didn't end up with him, did she? She chose you. Both of you need to kiss and make up before the sun goes down. All can be fixed with a few simple but very powerful words: "I am sorry. I was a jealous schmuck. Will you forgive me?"

The next time she goes to a high school reunion, get on that plane with her. No man in his right mind—even an old boyfriend—will put the moves on your woman if you're right by her side. Especially if you're carrying a buzz saw.

## Not Excited about Sex

**Q:** I've been faithful to my wife for our 15 years of marriage. I work hard, support her, and encourage her. But a big element is missing—sex. In our first few months of marriage, we had sex, but I always had this feeling that I was the only one excited about it. She just let it happen as if it was something she had to do—like clean a closet—instead of something that was wonderful and exciting.

I can't tell you how disappointing that is. I long for her to touch me because she wants to and likes to, instead of with the attitude of, "Okay, I'll do this because he seems to like it." What am I doing wrong? We haven't had sex for over a year, and I can feel the pressure building inside.

**A:** Let me ask you a blunt question. Have you ever talked with each other about sex—actually said the word? Have you talked about what each of you likes and doesn't like, and why she seems reluctant to have sex? My guess is that you haven't. You don't dare upset the applecart, and her reticence to even engage in the act tells me she doesn't want to either. So you both sit with the elephant between you on the couch.

It's as rare for a couple to have a lousy sex life and good communication as it is for a couple to have lousy communication and a good sex life. The two go hand in hand. If you're struggling in this area, though, why the mask? Why can't you come clean with your wife and tell her what you need? Chances are, there are unsettled issues in your relationship or perhaps in your wife's past. Has she experienced sexual abuse?

If your wife refuses to talk with you about why she doesn't engage in sex, you need to book an appointment with a trusted marriage counselor. Find a counselor who wants to get rid of you. Yes, you read that right. If you find one who is willing to give you a few sessions to get to the heart of what's going on, you'll be in better shape than if you find a counselor who wants to hang around for a couple of years.

Your marriage is too precious not to fight for it—every aspect of it. If your car wasn't running properly, you'd take it to a mechanic, right? Well, if the engine of your marriage is running rough, or not running at all, wouldn't you take it to a marriage mechanic? So make that appointment.

## I Talk . . . but She Says I Don't

**Q:** My wife says I don't talk enough—that our communication isn't very satisfying. I don't get it. I do talk to her, about a lot of things. What else am I supposed to say?

**A:** If your wife doesn't think you communicate very well, join another billion men around the world. Most men don't know what is satisfying to women when it comes to communication. You see, there are six levels of communication in marriage. What turns a woman on sexually is when you get to the sixth level and stay there regularly.

After you read each level, ask yourself, *Do I communicate with my wife on that level?*

Level 1: This is the least satisfying level of communication. You ask your spouse, "What was your day like?" and she says, "Oh, it was fine." Or, "Honey, would you please pass the pepper?" At this level, there's no possibility for conflict. Neither of you are engaged emotionally with each other.

Level 2: You share facts with each other. "Hey, what happened to the weather? The sun was supposed to shine today." Or, "Did you read about what happened in Africa yesterday?"

A lot of couples stay on levels 1 and 2 and wonder why their communication isn't satisfying. It's because they haven't taken the risk to go beyond those levels.

Level 3: You share your opinions with each other. This is the level at which you have most of your arguments, which is why many couples chicken out and stay at levels 1 and 2. Most husbands and wives have different opinions about everything based on how they were raised, their belief systems, their personalities, their goals, etc. However, the arguments you have in level 3 are designed to help you go deeper in your relationship. Those fights are actually drawing you toward deeper intimacy, because they lead you to levels 4 through 6. Isn't that a good reason to fight?

Level 4: You start sharing your deep feelings—how you really feel about something. For example, the argument you had in level 3 made you feel sad or discouraged or fearful. Men who reach level 4 in their communication find their wives more sexually responsive. That's because whenever a husband shares his feelings or heart with his wife, she feels closer to him. And that makes her want to be close to him in every way.

Level 5: You share your needs. "Honey, you know what I really need from you?" Share that you crave more passion in bed—or whatever your desire is. The bonds formed by spouses who talk at this level are hard to break.

Level 6: You uncover and discover what your spouse truly believes—what perspective of life does she have, and why? How would she respond to the phrase, "I only count when . . ."? What does she believe about life? Her career? Your future together? How the past influences her? At this sixth level is when you can truly say, "I love you with all my heart. I believe in you. I crave being with you. I'm fascinated by you. There's no one I'd rather spend time with than you." And that fascination leads you to incredible marital intimacy and the kind of bed-shaking sex you definitely wouldn't want to tell your mama about. Trust me, get to level 6 and you'll soar to amazing heights in the bedroom.

What's the best place to start? Where you are right now. Just edge to the next level, and then the next, and then the next. You'll be grateful you did, and so will your spouse.

## He's a Workaholic

**Q:** My guy's a workaholic, always driving to get to the next level in his career. Frankly, I feel left in the dust. Whenever I attempt to broach the subject, he shuts down and won't talk to me. Our house gets really tense.

I remember the days early in our marriage where sex was fun and spontaneous. Now it feels like something he ticks off his checklist once a week, on Saturday nights. There's no warmth, and he doesn't say anything when we make love. I miss the words he used to whisper to me as he nuzzled my neck. How can I tell him that I want the man I fell in love with back, without offending him and getting the ice treatment?

**A:** The two most important sex organs you have are your heart and your brain. For a husband and wife to grow together, you need to share things from the heart. That requires time together and a lot of communication since men and women handle emotions very differently. You also need to use your brain to decide to love. Love is not a onetime choice; it's a continual decision to treat your spouse as your top priority.

Right now your husband is choosing work over you and your family. But you have to understand why he's doing it. Many men have—and should have—a provider mentality. It's their love language, so to speak. All the time he's working those extra hours to get to the top, he's telling himself, *I'm doing all this work for my wife and the kids. They'll never have to worry about money. I can give them the best of everything.*

Some men also go after their career with gusto because they fear being left behind or losing their job in a cutthroat industry—a very real possibility in today's world. If so, maybe it's time to discuss a job change.

There might also be unsettled issues at home or in your relationship that prompt him to focus on work. Is home a place he likes to be, or is he avoiding it because the environment is tense? If so, now's the time to unravel those issues. A woman cannot live long without warmth from her husband. Feeling you're something to be checked off his to-do list will only cause resentment on your part.

It's important that you and your husband clear the decks to talk about what's really going on. Are there issues between you that have been swept under the rug for a while? If so, it's time to pick up that rug and shake it to see what falls out. Examine those issues in the light of day.

Why is your husband driven to be a workaholic? His background can play a big part. Is it because he felt he could never live up to his parents' expectations of him, so now he's trying doubly hard? Is it because you've overextended yourselves on your mortgage and the life mantra his father instilled in him was, "If you don't provide for your family, you're worthless"?

You need to hit the pause button on life and figure out what's driving him. Then come up with solutions. Being a workaholic on a specific project for a certain amount of time is one thing—there's an end in sight. But if it's a way of life, both of you and your relationship will suffer.

## My Husband Is "Wife-Deaf"

**Q:** Every time I try to have a discussion with my husband about things that are important, he retreats. I feel like I'm talking to a wall. Nothing gets accomplished, and I get frustrated. Worse, he gets that steely-eyed look that drives me crazy. He might be sitting there in his La-Z-Boy, but he's sure not listening. How can I talk so he'll listen? I really want to know.

**A:** There's a huge difference between men and women. When a woman sees her marriage as worth fighting for and wants to get her point across, she will talk and talk and talk. Yet the sheer volume of her words has the opposite result she intends for her husband. He hears her talking and either tunes her out or turns down her volume, like he would a bad radio show with static.

However, the answer isn't simply for you to stop talking. When a woman quits talking, she also quits trying, which means she withdraws from the marriage. *So*, you think, *he's not going to listen.*

248

*Well, I'm not going to get hurt any more than I already am.* You lock up your heart and leave your husband on the other side of the door. What does a guy think when you're quiet? *Oh, good, she's finally over that. Problem solved. I can relax now.* He doesn't realize it's because you've quit trying and you've installed a hefty locked door between you.

Please don't go there for either of your sakes. Instead, figure out how to talk so he'll listen.

When you approach your husband now, what do you say and what tone do you use? If you say something like, "Honey, we've got to talk" in a firm voice, your turtle will pull his head into his shell. He'll especially do it if you're emotional—tears are not something a man is comfortable with. Female emotions easily overwhelm and frustrate him. If he senses combativeness and purpose in your voice, he's not going there. In fact, he's not saying anything. He knows he won't win the war, so he doesn't even want to get into the skirmish. That turtle will simply tuck tightly into his shell until he resembles an impenetrable rock.

Women are naturally more gifted with words, and they can use them easily to get what they want. Men can't even hope to keep up when a woman gets on a roll. So what do we do? We retreat from a potential battlefield to safe ground. For many of us, when you talk, we hear, "Blah, blah, blah, blah," because we purposefully stop our ears if the flow of words is too great.

But what if you said, "You know, honey, I was thinking about the fact we're going to need to find a car soon. Yesterday was the third time I had to interrupt your workday to come pick me up when the engine died. You're so good at solving puzzles and problems, I was hoping you could give some advice. Do you think we should pursue a one-year-old car, a seven-year-old car, or a new car? And what kind of car?"

Now you've got your guy's attention. He'll perk right up. Saying you interrupted his workday when your clunker died tells him you understand how hard he works to provide for the family. He loves to solve problems, and he wants to be your hero, just like he was when he rescued you yesterday. It's a great solution for both of you. It'll get him out of that comfy chair and launched into some research.

If you engage his interest in that way, a big part of your problem is already solved. Your guy is in your court without you having to harangue him. Not only will he be on the prowl to find that car, but he'll make sure the oil in your clunker gets changed and even will clean the bugs off the windshield for you.

And while he's researching cars on the internet, he might come across a great deal for a second honeymoon in Acapulco. You never know.

## When I Point Things Out to My Wife, She Says I'm Critical

**Q:** Little things I notice are important to me, and I tend to comment on them. But my wife calls my comments critical, and she gets upset. If I mention that the roast is overdone or not done enough, she takes it as a personal insult. I feel it's important to be honest about things. How can something be improved if I'm not allowed to say anything? Is there some way I should say it differently?

**A:** Let me guess. You're a firstborn and a perfectionist. You're always trying to improve on things. Problem is, sometimes others can take that differently from the way you intend—as you being critical of them. Your wife wants to please you, but if she can't get the roast done to your perfection, she feels like she's failed. You're thinking, *Hey, just cook the roast about 10 more minutes at 350 degrees, flip it to the other side, and cook it another 10 minutes at 425 degrees, and it would be perfectly browned.* Well then, sometime *you* try cooking the roast that way. When you realize how much work it is, and that it ties you to the kitchen when you have other things you need to do simultaneously, you might be singing a different tune and be more grateful to your wife for cooking the roast at all.

You see, it's all in the perspective.

If your wife gets a new dress for a dinner with your colleagues, you saying, "Honey, that shade of red doesn't quite go with your complexion" will only gain you a not-so-happy dinner companion. She cared enough about you and how she looks in front of your colleagues that she worked hard to find that special dress. The least you can say is, "Wow, honey, you got a new dress. Thanks for going the extra mile for this dinner that's so important to me." That's honest. You don't always have to say everything you think. If you tell her the dress is unflattering, she will translate that to thinking she's ugly and not good enough for you. You may be criticizing the dress, but it comes across to your wife like you're criticizing her.

Criticism is deadly in marriage. It will wound her heart and make her bitter and resentful. Criticism is rooted in insecurity, fear, anger, and control. So I need to ask, why do you find yourself always critical? Did you grow up in a home where your every action was criticized? Did you have one or more dictatorial parents, who felt it was their right and privilege to pontificate on everything you did? If so, you grew up thinking that criticism is a normal part of a relationship, and you're acting out that same role in your marriage.

You're also a guy, so you're focused on getting a job done in the quickest way possible. Saying something straightforwardly works well for you at your job, so you think it also works at home. Your logic is, *If I tell my wife the meat is undercooked, next time she'll cook it more.* You think you're offering her a practical, helpful suggestion.

But every time you aim a criticism at her, it hammers a nail into her sense of well-being. And your criticism will indeed make her cook that meat more. In fact, she'll stand right in front of that oven and watch the roast burn to a crisp before she serves it to you with a flourish.

Women are relational. They care what others think and about how they look. Words matter greatly to your wife, and she longs to hear words of affirmation. "Honey, wow, I love your new dress. It's a different shade than I've seen you wear before. Where did you find it? It seems to suit you." Or, "Mmm, I smell roast. I love the way you try new recipes. What did you do differently this time?" Another appreciative sniff. "Smells like rosemary and garlic."

Now that's putting your perfectionism and your keen nose toward a good purpose.

And when you two eat that roast, because she's been appreciated by you, she may say to herself, "Hmm, I think the roast is a little underdone. Maybe I should . . ." Let her come up with the solution herself without you pronouncing it.

The words you choose to say with the one you love make all the difference. Are they filled with criticism? Or are they kind and tenderhearted? If you don't address your critical nature, your wife will wall herself off, brick by brick, to insulate herself against your comments.

When you do have to say something that isn't pleasant, it's important to separate the person you love from the event. For example, let's say your wife dings the front bumper of the car and scrapes up the garage wall for the second time in three months. Saying, "What on earth is the matter with you? You have a license, but you really need to learn how to drive" is not helpful. What if you said instead, "Honey, I know that spatial orientation isn't your thing. What can we do to help you judge the distance between the front of the car and the garage wall so we can keep any car repairs to a minimum? Any ideas?"

Either way, you're addressing the issue—the bumper and garage wall got damaged. You're a perfectionist, so things like that drive you nuts. However, criticizing merely drives a wall (literally) between you. Acknowledging the problem happened and needs to be resolved, then asking to think of the best way to keep it from happening in the future, is a much better way to go.

Friends of mine came up with a great solution, by the way. He, being the perfectionist, hung a bright yellow Ping-Pong ball from the ceiling of the garage so that all she has to do is drive the car up into the garage. When the Ping-Pong ball hits her front windshield, she stops. Problem solved. No more dings to the car or scrapes on the garage wall. And every time she looks at that yellow ball, she smiles because she remembers how much her husband loves her. He didn't criticize; he didn't yell when the accidents occurred. He came up with a solution that worked for both of them.

Next time, before you open your mouth to criticize, think, *What yellow Ping-Pong ball solution could work in this case?*

Then you'll be talking in a way that your wife will be happy to hear.

## Need Some Romance . . . and a Word Here or There

**Q:** My husband doesn't really talk when he gets home from work. When I ask him, "Hey, honey, how was your day?" I just get an "okay" or "fine." Then he's off to change clothes. About the only conversation I get from him over dinner is, "Oh, would you have time to get the oil changed in the car tomorrow?" Wow, now that's romantic and gets my heart fluttering.

After the evening news, all of a sudden he gives me that little eyebrow wiggle. I know what that means, but honestly, by then I'm so ticked I don't want anything to do with it. Even when we do have sex, it's silent. It's like I'm a vending machine. Put in a quarter and *ka-ching!* Out comes the sex. For once I'd like him to whisper sweet words in my ear. How can I encourage things in that direction?

**A:** Men can have a day from you-know-where and still turn on instantly. Just the sight of you can get Mr. Happy flying high. But women need and love little things, like conversation, cuddling, and a flower here or there. Your husband needs a 101 course on what women like. And you know who he needs to hear it from? You.

You can get ticked and do nothing. Or you can use that ticked-off-ness to gain the type of attention and talking you long for—a heart connection that will keep sweet somethings flowing out of your husband's mouth.

Be kind but honest. "Honey, I know you want sex. I want to share that with you too. But I also crave romance. Here's what I'd like you to do. . . ."

We guys aren't naturally good at romance. We aren't naturally good at talking. But we're very good at doing what our wives tell us to do, when they say it nicely. Applaud us afterward and we're like a seal that gets thrown a fish after a great performance—ready to go another round to do whatever you want us to do. Just try it and see.

### Am I Really Needed? Sometimes I Wonder . . .

**Q:** My wife is a very capable person who keeps our house running admirably. Sometimes too much, though. When I walk in after work, I sometimes wonder if I'm needed for anything other than my paycheck. I know that sounds whiny and insecure, but that's the way I feel sometimes.

How can I convey to my wife that I need her and the kids to need me? That I want to be a part of things and help to solve problems, rather than have them all solved by the time I get home?

**A:** We men are, at our core, problem solvers. Take that away from us and we don't quite know what to do with ourselves. Our three highest needs are to be wanted, to be needed, and to be respected. Sounds like you're at the very least not feeling needed or respected. If you're feeling like you're not wearing any pants in the family, that makes you feel naked and vulnerable, and it's doubtful you're fulfilled in your role as a male either.

Talk with your wife and tell her, "Honey, I so appreciate what you do around the house. You're a whiz with the kids and a super manager. I really want to be a part of things—to help you and the kids. In fact, that desire is what drives me to come home as fast as possible every night. What can I do to help you? To make things easier and simpler? I know you're going 24/7, but I want to carry some of the load. It's important to me as a man and as your husband. Can I pick up groceries for you on my way home?"

Give some practical suggestions and then make sure you follow through. If your spouse is a super manager, it's likely she's a firstborn or only child who thrives on control. She may feel uncomfortable if she's not in control. But if you do what you say you're going to, when you're going to, she'll trust you and grow comfortable in counting on you.

## Starving for Conversation

**Q:** My husband is really quiet and set in his ways. The only person he talks to, it seems, is me. I wish sometimes he were more social, or at least that he talked more. Sometimes I feel like I'm starving for conversation at home. It's hard for me to get close sexually if I don't even know what he's thinking or feeling. And when we do have sex, he seems to enjoy it, but he doesn't talk then either. How can I get the man to talk?

**A:** Do something for me. Count the number of friends you have that you talk to regularly. Now count the number of people your husband talks to. One finger will do it. You're the only friend he talks to. That's like most of us males—we keep our secrets close to our chests and most people at arm's length. But you? What a lucky woman. You've weaseled your way into his heart and lodged there.

Women use three and a half times as many words as men do on any given day. So by the time evening comes and he strolls in that door, he's already used up his word count at work. You've still got a lot left to go.

What do you do when he gets home? Do you pepper him with questions? If so, stop asking questions. Just greet him with a hug and kiss and tell him how much you love him. Let him smell dinner—even if it's only a microwave meal. Even better, tell him one thing you appreciate about him each day.

When he does finally talk, don't fire questions back at him. Instead, say, "Sounds like you've had quite a long day. Tell me more about it. I'd love to know." You'll be amazed at how your reticent husband will start spilling his thoughts and feelings to you.

Project accomplished. All it takes is an understanding of males and a little sensitivity on your part.

# *Friday*

## *Spice It Up!*

Why variety really is the zest in the marital recipe . . . especially when it comes to the bedroom.

### Boring in Bed

**Q:** My husband is a sweet guy, but he is sooo boring in bed. Whatever works one time he does over and over and over. How can I get him to be more experimental?

**A:** It's simple. Many men eat the same breakfast every day—myself included—and that doesn't bother us one bit. But you women? You like variety.

That sweet guy wants to please you but has no clue how to do it. If something worked one time, he thinks, *Oh, hey, she liked that, so I'll always do it.* All he needs is some creative suggestions from you. Whisper in his ear, "Hey, honey, I've got an idea of something we can do right now . . . something new I'd like to try." A little swivel of your hips, a crooked finger, and he'll get the message. One "come hither" look is enough to get any red-blooded male ready and willing to try anything different. He just may need you to come up with some options. And when he sees you like different things at different times, don't be surprised if your lover comes up with some ideas of his own.

## Masturbation—Okay or Not?

**Q:** Is it okay to masturbate, or not? I'm in the mood a lot more than my spouse, who has a much lower energy level. Sometimes I really need sexual release. What should I do during those times?

**A:** Let me tell you a story. A woman called me once. She was panicking because she'd caught her husband masturbating in the shower. "Dr. Leman, what do I do?" she asked. "He's a sexual pervert."

I told her that 90 percent of men masturbate. The other 10 percent are lying. And a lot of women also masturbate. I said, "You know how I'd handle that situation if I were a woman? I'd strip right in front of my husband and say, 'Honey, can I be of service to you?'"

Frankly, there are times when you or your spouse may need to receive loving expressions manually. Can we talk turkey? It's called a hand job, and it's very permissible and pleasurable for both of you.

There are also times when you just want a quickie. A little something to tide you over until you can engage in a longer period of cuddling and sex. Sometimes the wife needs it; sometimes the husband needs it. The goal is to satisfy each other when you're too pooped to whoop or you simply don't have the time.

Spouses will have differing energy levels and expectations when it comes to the frequency of sex and what kind of sex.

This is especially true when one of the spouses is going through a difficult time, whether emotionally or physically. Yes, masturbation will take care of physical release when you're keyed up. But it won't satisfy the craving you have for the warmth and intimacy of the sexual experience within marriage. It never can, since masturbation is something you do by yourself, with yourself. And no, you won't go senile. You won't get dementia. You won't go blind. Hair won't grow between your fingers. All those are flat-out lies.

A person is not simply a sexual organ. You have a heart, emotions, a sexual drive, and an imagination. The imagination is where things get tricky. When real people become connected to the act of masturbation, then it becomes a major problem because it confuses relationships and puts a focus on aspects of sex that may never be satisfied. If you are thinking of your spouse when you masturbate, your sexual drive is staying between you and your spouse. However, as you masturbate, the need to do it more and to do it differently will kick in. You will find yourself imagining doing things sexually that your spouse may be uncomfortable doing with you. Or you may begin fantasizing someone else doing those things to you, and then you commit emotional adultery.

So here's what I'd suggest. Talk with your spouse before you've reached a point where you feel like you're going to explode sexually if you don't masturbate. Be honest about your desire for more sex. Say, "Honey, could we come up with some options together for when I feel like that? I love you so much, and what you need and want is important to me." By doing that, you open the door for discussion. Your spouse should be willing to push himself or herself a bit to offer more frequent sex. If that doesn't work, try other options. Have your spouse bring you to a climax by stroking and rubbing your genitals. That way he or she isn't breaking a sweat, but you're getting the release you desperately need . . . with your spouse right by your side.

The truth is, we're sexual people, and in marriage there are different strokes for different folks. Don't masturbate alone. Tell your spouse your needs, and when she doesn't feel like going all the way, the reliable old hand job can do the trick.

### Orgasms—One or Multiple?

**Q:** My husband read somewhere that women can have multiple orgasms, and he's trying to make it happen for me. But honestly, I'm happy with one. Attempting to make more happen is too much. Sometimes it's even painful because the areas he touches are sensitive. How can I explain to him that one orgasm is enough?

**A:** It's not surprising your husband is competitive. Men are competitive. But in this case, he's playing marital Whac-A-Mole. Your husband is thinking, *Well, if it's possible to bring her more pleasure, I'm sure going to do it.* His driven nature has kicked in, and that man of yours wants to provide you with the best in all areas of life, including lovemaking. Well, good for him.

Some women love having multiple orgasms in any lovemaking session. Others may not be able to have them, feel that more than one is too intense or painful (as it is for you), or decide simply that they don't want more than one. What you're seeking is the basking in the afterglow of one orgasm and relaxing with your husband, feeling the closeness and relationship. So tell him that. Affirm his superior lovemaking skills in bringing you to a climax. What's important is that you are both happy and satisfied in what you're doing together—regardless of what some online or magazine "expert" says.

But you have to be straightforward with your husband. Otherwise he's going to keep trying to give you what he's been told is a better, sexier experience—you having multiple orgasms. *If that guy says he can cause his wife to have multiple orgasms, I can too,* your husband is thinking. So gently correct his thinking, tell him he's all the man you'll ever need, and lead him by the hand to your bedroom to show him just that.

### Squeezing In the Time

**Q:** How can a couple have an exciting sex life when their lives are so busy? Between work, the kids, and the plumbing leaks, my wife and I barely have time to squeeze in an "I love you," much less anything else. Ideas?

**A:** Let me ask you: When was the last time you surprised your wife, took her someplace special, and made all the arrangements? When was the last time you gave her a card or sent her a tender text—from your heart to hers? Have you ever used a bar of soap to make a big heart on the bathroom mirror, with "I love you" written inside it? Do you tell her every night one thing that you appreciate about her?

Love isn't just a tingly, euphoric feeling you drum up when you have time in your schedule. It's the small, daily actions that go on until you get your picture in the paper, looking all wrinkly like a raisin, as you celebrate your fiftieth wedding anniversary.

I've been right there in the trenches with you, especially when my kids were young. Life is busy. It's hard to find time for each other. That's why you have to work hard to prioritize sex and marital intimacy.

Take your bride on an overnighter. Do something exciting. Send an email that says, *Great news! I've arranged for the kids to be gone tonight to Grandma and Grandpa's. And I have some special hors d'oeuvres planned for both you and me to wear. See you right after work.*

That wife of yours might have a terrible headache from a teething baby or an emotional adolescent. But that email will make her smile all day and put her in the mood to want you to hurry home. That's what sex ought to be—something to anticipate. All it takes is a little thought and planning and a few kind words.

So make time for marital intimacy. Get a babysitter or swap with another couple, and go out. Even spend a few bucks on a hotel sometimes. You spend money on other things, like Netflix, right? Then why not invest some money every month on your spouse? Believe me, it will pay better dividends than Netflix.

### Nonsexual Touch, Foreplay, Sex—What's What?

**Q:** I read somewhere that there's a difference between nonsexual touch, foreplay, and sex, and that all three are important—especially to a woman. But I'm not quite sure what the difference is. I've always thought of sex as kind of an "all or nothing" experience. Could you help me out?

**A:** You bet, and good for you for asking. I appreciate inquiring minds.

Nonsexual touch is all the little gestures you do for your wife during the day—kissing her when you leave for work, caressing her cheek, rubbing the small of her back, and massaging her feet at night—that make deposits in her love bank. This is the type of touch that tells her, "You're special." It's not a means to an end—having sex with her.

Foreplay is the sensual stroking, the touch, that leads to sexual play and climax. It *is* a means to an end—the act of having sex.

Sex is the physical act of intercourse or oral sex—genital to genital or mouth to genital.

In order to feel ready for foreplay and desire the culmination in the act of sex, a woman needs lots of nonsexual touch during the day. That leads her to feel secure that you love her and have eyes only for her. Then when you move close to her and start the foreplay, she thinks, *Wow, what an incredible man I married. Just today he . . .* and she flashes back to the sweet ways you showed you cared for her.

### It's All about the Presentation

**Q:** My wife and I used to have great sex, and a lot of it. But we've slowed down recently now that we've been married a year. The other day, when I was reaching for her in the kitchen, she turned toward me and said, "Nuh-uh, not until you take a shower." She's never told me that before. In the past we've made love even after I came in the door sweaty after playing basketball. Am I losing my touch? Is she getting too fussy? Or what?

**A:** There's a simple fix. Go take a shower. Then go back and engage that wife of yours in some hot sex that will require you both to take another shower . . . together.

During your first year of marriage, when hormones often run high, you were ready to jump in the sack at any time. Now, to get the juices stirring, your wife is making a simple request.

A simple request, yes, but strategically important. She might have put up with your sweaty body for the first year, but the enticement of dealing with that sticky and maybe aromatic sweat may be wearing a little thin.

You see, to women, presentation is everything. For example, you may not mind eating a peanut butter and jelly sandwich for lunch. You don't even mind if the sandwich is squished inside the plastic bag and the bag is sticky with jelly. It's food and all good. You don't care what it looks like, as long as it fills your belly. But your wife? If she takes a look at that sandwich with the jelly oozing out, she's likely to wrinkle her nose and, with thumb and forefinger pinched on the bag, give it the toss-ola into the trash. The presentation is no longer pretty, and thus it doesn't look interesting to her. She'd rather go hungry than eat something that doesn't attract her eye.

Just about anyone can biologically perform the act of sexual intercourse, just as anyone can make a peanut butter and jelly sandwich. But if you want a gourmet meal with beautiful presentation, you need to find a chef. A good sexual "chef" does the same thing.

A loving husband cares about the presentation because his wife does. To truly engage your wife's senses, you need to be fresh smelling, tender, romantic, and experimental. That means you move from the peanut butter and jelly sandwich sexual experience to the gourmet dinner experience, complete with beautiful colors arranged tastefully on the plate. And because it's so pleasing to your wife's eye, what a difference there is in taste to her!

So let me ask you, is your presentation beautiful and exciting? Do you dim the lights, put a chocolate or a rose on her pillow, take a shower so you smell fresh? Such gestures mean everything to women.

Taking a shower is a small thing—a little water, soap, a minute of your time. But it'll change your body from a squished peanut butter and jelly sandwich into a gourmet plate for your wife to sample.

I guarantee it'll be worth all the effort you give it, Mr. Gourmet Chef.

## ASAP Sex

**Q:** After we had sex, the next day I noticed my wife had a bruise . . . caused by me. I felt really bad, because I knew I'd hurt her. I'm a tough guy who had to fight my way through childhood for survival, but I don't ever want to treat my wife roughly. How can I control myself even in the height of passion? And what do I tell her?

**A:** The first thing you can do for both of you is to take a look at your attitude toward your wife and toward sex in general. Do you see her as someone to conquer, like the people you had to fight in childhood? Or do you see her as the delicate flower she is, who deserves to be treated like a queen by you? Do you see sex as merely a release of physical tension and something you deserve—something your wife should do for you?

There's no excuse for treating a woman roughly—ever. For a woman to feel loved, secure, and protected, sex needs to happen ASAP: as slow as possible. You might be ready to go the second you hear the shower running and think about her naked. But a woman is like a delicate orchid that has to be cultivated, watered, and handled very carefully. Her clitoris has to be touched ever so softly. She needs to be stroked all over gently to reach a point where she wants to be joined with you.

Even more, she's not mechanical like you. What she likes on Saturday she won't like on Tuesday. You're logical—do A, then B, and you get C. She's mysterious—you have to figure her out. Then again, that's what attracted you to her in the first place, right?

She was drawn to your masculinity, your strength. But that strength always needs to be shielded in gentleness and control with your wife.

Like orchids need the right mix of water and light, she needs affection and communication from you. She needs to be embraced by you nonsexually first, then slowly drawn toward the act of sex. If you gently bring her along toward that climax, she'll come to a place where she says, "Oh, don't stop! Keep going!" Then all of a sudden she's a cheerleader in the experience.

For a woman to fully enjoy sex and come to a powerful orgasm, she needs a gentle leader—a man who exerts control over himself, as much as he's physically craving the culmination and release of ejaculation. There's a time for a bit more pressure on certain body parts, but never roughness. She's a rare orchid—if you touch her too hard, you'll bruise her petals.

Try this. Enter lovemaking with the attitude of *I want to please my wife*. Go as far as she wants to go. Only as deep as she wants to go. Explore ways to touch her that will make her groan in pleasure. If you do, both of you will have a powerful sexual experience.

As for what to do next? Go to your wife and say humbly, "Oh, honey, I'm so sorry I got carried away and caused that bruise. I never want to hurt you in that way again." Talk about what you'd like to do differently next time to safeguard against that.

Then practice it next time ASAP—as slow as possible. Be a good lover, a slow lover, a gentle lover.

### Anal Sex—Okay or Not?

**Q:** I'm just wondering, is anal sex okay? I've read about it as an option for couples to experiment with, and my husband would like for us to try it. I'm not sure. What do you think?

**A:** In regards to experimenting with sex as a married couple, there are very few places where I'll draw the line. But I do draw the line at anal sex. Anal sex, to put it bluntly, is not only wrong; it's also not good for you physically or emotionally. The rectum was not designed by God Almighty to be used in such a manner, and infection and tears in delicate places can happen as a result.

This is one time where you need to give your husband a flat-out no. "No, I don't want to do that. I'm not comfortable with it." If he presses again, ask, "Why is engaging in anal sex so interesting and important to you? Are there other sexual things you'd like to try that we haven't discussed?"

You might find out that your husband has a few perverted ideas about sex. If so, ask him where he got those ideas. Did he secretly explore sexual stimulation because he grew up in a rigid environment—a home where sex was something that was nasty, dirty, and not discussed? Or was he sexually abused as a child in any way—either by the same sex or the opposite sex—or introduced to pornography? Does he think that the only things that make sex pleasurable are encounters where they feel nasty and dirty?

Why is he not interested in "normal sex"—stroking, fondling, intercourse, oral sex, etc.? Those are key questions.

Most of all, it would be a shame to turn what God Almighty created as the most intense, exciting act in marriage into something mentally and emotionally deplorable and also physically harmful. So I beg you, don't go there.

### How to Fix Boring Sex

**Q:** Sex isn't as exciting as it used to be. I'm not as turned on by my wife as I used to be, and from the lack of initiation on her side, I'm certain she feels the same way. I want us to get those old feelings back, but is that possible once you've been married awhile? Or should we just accept things the way they are? Every Saturday night we watch a movie, make love, and then fall asleep. It's kind of what we do on Saturdays. We jokingly refer to it as our "sex day." But sex has lost all spontaneity. Any suggestions to make things more exciting?

**A:** It's great you make love every Saturday night. A lot of couples would be grateful to step into your shoes and know that they have Saturday night every week by themselves.

But you definitely have to address the routine, boring part of it. Shake things up a little. Have you tried quickies during the week, whenever you can fit them in? Then you can make Saturday the night you take it slow and really enjoy yourself.

If the movie is lulling you into boredom, strip to your underwear and have your wife sit on your lap on that couch. Snuggle under a blanket and start stroking each other. I guarantee you won't make it past a few scenes before you're ripping that underwear off and going for it. You won't even care you missed the rest of the movie.

Or skip the movie altogether. Cook dinner together naked and see what happens. Get in the tub and explore each other's bodies underwater. All it takes is a little creativity to spice things up.

I'm sure you can come up with more ideas once you get started.

## Sexual Fantasies

**Q:** I find myself having sexual fantasies all the time. Is that normal, or do I need some psychiatric help?

**A:** If you have sexual fantasies, your sexual drive may be very high—higher than your spouse's. That means you may not be getting sex as much as you'd like to in your marriage. There's nothing wrong with sexual fantasies if:

- They are about and focused on your spouse.
- They fall within normal bounds of acceptable sex, such as intercourse, oral sex, stroking, fondling, and cuddling your spouse.
- You share them with your spouse so that together you can brainstorm new and exciting ways to be intimate.

It's when sexual fantasies step outside those very important points that problems occur. It's a red flag if you daydream of having sex with someone else, or you dream of having dangerous sex (such as anal sex) to spice things up.

If you need more sex with your spouse and more variety, talk with him or her. Share your needs and your fantasies. See what you can come up with together. Who knows? Your sexual fantasy might end up being your spouse's favorite kind of sex. Why not experiment and try it out?

## Oral Sex—Okay or Not?

**Q:** I'd really like to try oral sex. The idea excites me, because I like to try new things. But my husband isn't comfortable with it. He likes sex "the good, old-fashioned way," he says. "The one way God intended it." To my husband, that means the same way every time. No variety. I crave variety, exploring new things. Is oral sex okay or not?

**A:** Is oral sex okay? Are you kidding me? It's *great*! However, here's the bad news. It's not great if your spouse doesn't agree. Is it permissible? Yes. But love never demands its own way. It will only work for you if you and your husband are comfortable experimenting with it. For many people, it's an acquired taste (and yes, I did mean that pun). I know because people tell me about it, and they range from newlyweds to those celebrating their thirtieth anniversary.

If you still want to explore the idea, ask your husband if he would be willing for you to try it on him one time, just as an experiment. Assure him you don't expect him to try it out on you. You will honor his wishes.

After that man of yours gets a little taste of what your mouth feels like on his penis, he might just change his tune as he orbits to Jupiter and Mars a bit before crashing back down to earth. At his heart, your lover wants to please you—he wants to see you writhe in excitement. After your little rendezvous, he might think, *Hmm, if I tried oral sex on her, I wonder how she'd respond.* And he's off and running with the seed planted for a later lovemaking session.

269

When he does awkwardly try oral sex for the first time, just watch him pat himself on the back psychologically. *Well, would you look at that? I did that to her—yeah, I did. Just call me "stud."* Once couples try out oral sex, many of them are surprised. Even the most reticent of spouses can find oral sex an exciting alternative to spice things up in the bedroom.

Try it with your guy and see.

## From Robot Sex to Wow Sex

**Q:** I'm a logical, methodical guy. I love it when things are predictable and you can do them step-by-step. Most of the time that works well for me, but my wife of 12 years told me last week that having sex with me is like having sex with a robot. Ouch. I had no idea she felt that way. She said she didn't want to hurt my feelings or she'd have told me earlier. I wish she would have. I'm a problem solver. I like to figure things out and get them right. Well, now I want to get making love to my wife right. Problem is, I don't know where to start. Help me out?

**A:** Most of us guys are logical and methodical. We think sex is like a football playbook. You do this, then this, and get that result. But with women, who like variety and change emotions faster than you change your underwear, doing things step-by-step isn't the formula to success. The most important thing is that you get behind her eyes to see how she views life. What kind of day has she had? Would she like a foot rub or a back rub instead of sex? Would she like a little more foreplay before you go for the goal?

If I said to your bride, "Hey, tell me what your sex life is like with your husband," would she say you're predictable? "Well . . . he always starts here, does this, and ends up there."

Now that's exciting. If I were a woman, I'd be looking forward to that too—knowing exactly what was going to happen and when.

Let me ask you something. After you watch a football game, would you want to watch that same game over and over and over, four or five times a week, knowing exactly what every play would be? What every player would do? Who made the final touchdown to win the game?

I doubt it. After a while you'd be asleep in that easy chair.

That's what's happening in your sex life. Knowing what's going to happen has lulled your wife to sleep. Yes, she's there with you, but using a sexual playbook of rules will never excite her.

She wants to feel loved. She wants to experience new things with you when you have sex.

So tuck away that playbook. The next time you have sex, start touching her in a completely different area than you usually do. Watch your wife perk up, shiver, and open her eyes wide. Stroke her all over her body. Even better, let her guide your hands, and let them roam.

If you do that, your robot days are over. Not only will you get excited about trying new things because you'll see your wife's response, but she'll realize you're up for some variety and will try ideas of her own too.

It takes two to create sizzling sex—to go from robot sex to wow sex. So what are you waiting for?

# Epilogue

## The Best Night of Your Life Awaits

It's time to jump-start the dead battery, revive the ailing engine, and rev up your sex life to full throttle. I promise it'll be fun!

My bride is a classy woman. She loves five-fork restaurants, but in a pinch she will gladly enjoy a three-forker. She loves all those little forks. I hate them . . . with a passion. At most I'm a one-fork guy, and if it's plastic and I can throw it out without doing the dishes, all the better. In fact, I'm even happier with barbecued ribs at a Western joint where you can eat with your fingers and lick them.

But I want to be a good husband. I want to please my bride, and she likes beautiful presentation—the nice evenings out with all the little forks that drive me up the wall. So where do I take her? To the five-forker. By now I've been schooled at what to do. I take a look at the place setting and know I'm supposed to start from the outside fork and work my way in. So I do that, and most of the time I end up with the right fork for the right course.

273

Well, when our kids were young, I could tell my bride needed one of those classy evenings out, just the two of us. But she needed something more too, and I knew just what I had to do.

So I took her to a nice five-forker, and we had a leisurely dinner. Afterward I drove her to a resort hotel. She gave me "the look." If you're a man, you know the look I mean. It says, "What on earth are you up to? There is no way I'm going to like it."

"Leemey, what are we doing here?" she asked in the uppity tone that earned her the nickname Mrs. Uppington.

"We're going to go into the hotel," I said calmly.

She crossed her arms and gave me her best firstborn scowl. "I don't know what you've got in mind, but I am not getting out of the car. I don't have any luggage. I'm not going in there." She crossed her arms with a little *hmmmfft* for extra measure.

I'd call that an uncooperative spirit.

I got out of the car and walked around to open her door like the gentleman I am.

But she'd locked the door. I sighed to myself, since I had the car key. I unlocked the door and literally lifted her up out of the car. "C'mon, we're going in there."

Gentlemen, you'll really understand what I say next. Volumes can be spoken with body language. My bride stalked toward the hotel with a fiery determination. Translated, that meant, "Okay, I'm going to go, but you are not going to have any fun."

She marched up to the front entrance, but I tugged her toward a different door. "No, not that way, this way."

She scowled at me again, then her eyes widened. She saw a room key in my hand.

I let us into the hotel, walked with her down the hallway, and swiped the room card. We entered the room, and she gasped. There on the big bed were two books I'd purchased for her, as well as three sweetheart roses, symbolizing the three children we had at the time. You see, I'd sneaked in there earlier that day so it was all set up for her. I had even ordered room service—triple chocolate cake and a fresh pot of coffee. Two things I know she loves.

Yes, it was 10:30 at night, folks.

Some of you are saying, "Well, I hope the coffee was decaf."

Nope, it was regular. That's because I know my wife's a raccoon—she's up half the night. If she had her way, an early start to her day would be 1:00 in the afternoon. So it's no wonder she was sleep deprived with three young children who were on a completely different schedule.

And then I did one of the manliest things I've ever done. I told her, "Honey, I'll be back at one o'clock tomorrow afternoon to take you to a late breakfast." Then I left.

That room had a king-sized bed, and I could picture my wife reclining on top of it. It was an incredible opportunity for us to be together, to have out-of-this-world sex, but I passed on that.

Why? Because I had learned something very important as a husband. You have to do those kinds of things for your wife— gestures that make her feel loved and appreciated for who she is—not simply for the sex she can give you.

My wife needed to be by herself that night. She needed to re-group. She needed a time-out from the voices of the children she dearly loved. She needed to get lost in a good novel or two. And because I knew what she needed and I had her best in mind for the long term, I sacrificed what I would have loved in the present—wild, passionate sex with the woman I love. The woman I want to share every bit of my life with.

Seeing the world behind each other's eyes is why, even in our later years, my bride and I still experience sexual ecstasy. We had two more children after the three we had when I took her to that hotel. In fact, the last one we conceived when Sande was 48 and I was 50. So don't ever let anybody tell you that you can't have great sex once you pass midlife. That's simply not true.

But that kind of sexual intimacy is only possible when you declare with little gestures throughout the day, "You're important to me—not only in a sexual or intimate way but because no one means more to me than you. I want to make your life pleasurable. I want to be by your side until the end of our days."

That means, gentlemen, you step up to the plate and be a leader in a servant-hearted, loving way. You get behind your wife's eyes and see how she views and experiences life. You make it your mission to know your bride and carry out the small things that make her feel loved, protected, and cared for.

Ladies, that means you realize every day how much your husband needs to be needed and wanted—by you. He craves your respect in his unique role in your home, and he desires to be sexually fulfilled. The words you use make a tremendous difference in your marriage, especially because you have a masterful flow of language and his words are few.

When you put each other's needs first, make each other feel special, and prioritize your time as a couple—yes, even with kids in the mix—you'll be surprised at how sensual and exciting sex can be. You'll be more open to experimentation. Sex and marital intimacy will satisfy both of you and draw your hearts together, and you'll want more.

Every time I return from a speaking trip, the first face I want to see is my beaming bride's. I want to rush into her arms and reconnect physically. We call and text in between, but neither is the same as being with her in person.

Just as I know what Sande needs, she also knows the desires of my heart and that, as a baby of the family, I crave surprises. One birthday she shocked me with an amazing present she'd been saving for—a black 1950 Ford 50. Not only is it a classic, which I greatly appreciate, but it's also the make and model of the first car I ever owned, and thus just looking at it floods me with wonderful memories. Even more, Sande herself had taken the time to carefully research and find the car.

Our marriage is now 40-plus years old, but it's like that classic car—worth far more because of the time that's been invested in its upkeep, the engine parts that have been tweaked along the way, and the love that's kept the motor purring along in satisfaction.

Right now is your time to craft your marriage into a classic car that stands the test of time. It's time to jump-start the dead battery, revive the ailing engine, and rev up your sex life and marital intimacy to full throttle.

In fact, I hope you're giving each other the Bullwinkle the Moose look right now as you finish this book. As my best friend says, "It's not great sex unless you have to take a shower afterward."

And you can sure make that shower fun too.

# Notes

**Introduction: Vive la Différence!**

1. Richard J. Haier, Rex E. Jung, Ronald A. Yeo, Kevin Head, and Michael T. Alkire, "The Neuroanatomy of General Intelligence: Sex Matters," *NeuroImage* 25 (2005): 320–27, http://www.imaginggenetics.org/PDFs/2005_Haier_NeuroImage_SexdiffIQ.pdf.
2. "How Male and Female Brains Differ," *WebMD*, April 11, 2005, http://www.webmd.com/balance/features/how-male-female-brains-differ?page=3.

**Wednesday: Someone's in Bed with You . . .**

1. See Ephesians 4:26.

**Friday: Spice It Up!**

1. Song of Solomon 2:3; 5:1; 6:2–3; 7:2; 8:2.

# About Dr. Kevin Leman

An internationally known psychologist, radio and television personality, speaker, educator, and humorist, **Dr. Kevin Leman** has taught and entertained audiences worldwide with his wit and commonsense psychology.

The *New York Times* bestselling and award-winning author of over 50 titles, including *The Birth Order Book, Have a New Kid by Friday,* and *Sheet Music,* has made thousands of house calls through radio and television programs, including *Fox & Friends, The Real Story, The View,* Fox's *The Morning Show, Today, Morning in America, The 700 Club,* CBS's *The Early Show, Janet Parshall,* CNN, and *Focus on the Family.* Dr. Leman has served as a contributing family psychologist to *Good Morning America* and frequently speaks to schools and businesses, including Fortune 500 companies such as YPO, Million Dollar Round Table, Top of the Table, and other CEO groups.

Dr. Leman's professional affiliations include the American Psychological Association, SAG-AFTRA, and the North American Society of Adlerian Psychology. He received the Distinguished Alumnus Award (1993) and an honorary Doctor of Humane Letters degree (2010) from North Park University; and a bachelor's degree in psychology, and later his master's and doctorate degrees, as well as the Alumni Achievement Award (2003), from the University of Arizona. Dr. Leman is also the founder and chairman of the board of the Leman Academy of Excellence (www .lemanacademy.com).

Originally from Williamsville, New York, Dr. Leman and his wife, Sande, live in Tucson, Arizona, and have five children and four grandchildren.

For information regarding speaking availability, business consultations, seminars, webinars, or the annual "Wit and Wisdom" cruise, please contact:

Dr. Kevin Leman
P.O. Box 35370
Tucson, Arizona 85740
Phone: (520) 797-3830
Fax: (520) 797-3809
www.birthorderguy.com
www.drleman.com

Follow Dr. Kevin Leman on Facebook (facebook.com/DrKevin Leman) and on Twitter (@DrKevinLeman). Check out the free podcasts at birthorderguy.com/podcast.

# Resources by Dr. Kevin Leman

**Nonfiction Books for Adults**

*Have a New Kid by Friday*

*The Birth Order Book*

*Have a Happy Family by Friday*

*Have a New Sex Life by Friday*

*Planet Middle School*

*Have a New Husband by Friday*

*Have a New Teenager by Friday*

*Have a New You by Friday*

*The Way of the Wise*

*Be the Dad She Needs You to Be*

*What a Difference a Mom Makes*

*Parenting the Powerful Child*

*Under the Sheets*

*Sheet Music*

*Making Children Mind without Losing Yours*

*It's Your Kid, Not a Gerbil!*

*Born to Win*

*Sex Begins in the Kitchen*

*7 Things He'll Never Tell You . . . But You Need to Know*

*What Your Childhood Memories Say about You*

*Running the Rapids*

*The Way of the Shepherd* (written with William Pentak)

*Becoming the Parent God Wants You to Be*

*Becoming a Couple of Promise*

*A Chicken's Guide to Talking Turkey with Your Kids about Sex* (written with Kathy Flores Bell)

*First-Time Mom*

*Step-Parenting 101*

*Living in a Stepfamily without Getting Stepped On*

*The Perfect Match*

*Be Your Own Shrink*

*Stopping Stress before It Stops You*

*Single Parenting That Works*

*Why Your Best Is Good Enough*

*Smart Women Know When to Say No*

## Fiction Books for Adults, with Jeff Nesbit

*The Worthington Destiny*

    *A Perfect Ambition*

    *A Powerful Secret*

    *A Primary Decision*

## Books for Children, with Kevin Leman II

*My Firstborn, There's No One Like You*
*My Middle Child, There's No One Like You*
*My Youngest, There's No One Like You*
*My Only Child, There's No One Like You*
*My Adopted Child, There's No One Like You*
*My Grandchild, There's No One Like You*

## DVD/Video Series for Group Use

*Have a New Kid by Friday*
*Making Children Mind without Losing Yours* (parenting edition)
*Making Children Mind without Losing Yours* (public school teacher edition)
*Value-Packed Parenting*
*Making the Most of Marriage*
*Running the Rapids*
*Single Parenting That Works*
*Bringing Peace and Harmony to the Blended Family*

## DVDs for Home Use

*Straight Talk on Parenting*
*Why You Are the Way You Are*
*Have a New Husband by Friday*
*Have a New You by Friday*
*Have a New Kid by Friday*

Available at 1-800-770-3830 • www.birthorderguy.com • www.drleman.com

# Have a new husband by Friday?
## Is that even possible?

OVER 100,000 COPIES SOLD

# Have a New♡ Husband by Friday

How to Change His
✓ Attitude
✓ Behavior &
✓ Communication in 5 Days

## Dr. Kevin Leman

*NEW YORK TIMES* BESTSELLING AUTHOR

Dr. Kevin Leman says it is. The *New York Times* bestselling author and relationship expert shows you how with his easy and accessible principles.